WHAT THE THUNDER SAID

WHAT THE THUNDER SAID

Reflections of a Canadian Officer in Kandahar

LIEUTENANT-COLONEL
JOHN CONRAD

Foreword by
Christie Blatchford

CANADIAN DEFENCE ACADEMY PRESS
KINGSTON

THE DUNDURN GROUP
TORONTO

Catalogue No. D2-246/2009E

Published by The Dundurn Group and Canadian Defence Academy Press in cooperation with the Department of National Defence, and Public Works and Government Services Canada.

Editor: Michael Carroll
Copy Editor: Nigel Heseltine
Designer: Jennifer Scott
Printer: Transcontinental

Library and Archives Canada Cataloguing in Publication

Conrad, John D.
    What the thunder said : reflections of a Canadian officer in Kandahar / John Conrad.

Issued also in French under title: Ce que dit le tonnerre.
Includes index.
ISBN 978-1-55488-408-7

    1. Afghan War, 2001- --Logistics--Canada. 2. Afghan War, 2001- --Participation, Canadian. 3. Canada--Armed Forces--Afghanistan. 4. Conrad, John D. 5. Afghan War, 2001- --Personal narratives, Canadian. I. Title.

DS371.413.C66 2009   958.104'7   C2009-900298-1

    2   3   4   5   13   12   11   10   09

 Conseil des Arts du Canada   Canada Council for the Arts  ONTARIO ARTS COUNCIL CONSEIL DES ARTS DE L'ONTARIO

We acknowledge the support of the **Canada Council for the Arts** and the **Ontario Arts Council** for our publishing program. We also acknowledge the financial support of the **Government of Canada** through the **Book Publishing Industry Development Program** and **The Association for the Export of Canadian Books**, and the **Government of Ontario** through the **Ontario Book Publishers Tax Credit** program and the **Ontario Media Development Corporation**.

Printed and bound in Canada
www.dundurn.com

Canadian Defence Academy Press
PO Box 17000 Station Forces
Kingston, Ontario, Canada
K7K 7B4

Dundurn Press   Gazelle Book Services Limited   Dundurn Press
3 Church Street, Suite 500   White Cross Mills   2250 Military Road
Toronto, Ontario, Canada   High Town, Lancaster, England   Tonawanda, NY U.S.A.
M5E 1M2   LA1 4XS   14150

To Master Corporal Raymond Arndt
and all the fine young men and women of
Task Force Afghanistan who have laid down
their lives in Afghanistan since 2002.

They shall not grow old as we
that are left grow old.
— Laurence Binyon, "For the Fallen," 1914

CONTENTS

FOREWORD
by Christie Blatchford

I still think of John Conrad as a native Newfoundlander, and probably always will. It is my experience that the most passionate and articulate Canadians come from that hard place, and from the first time I interviewed him, and he described the modern battlefield as akin to "water droplets on a walnut table, with the droplets the safe haven," I nearly fainted with pleasure at his use of the language. *What the Thunder Said* proves the point: John has brought his passion for logistics and shown how in the war in Afghanistan combat happens anywhere and everywhere, putting virtually every soldier, whether infantry or truck driver, squarely on the front line and smack in the midst of the fight.

Logistics and passion, even to those in the reborn Canadian Army (though not to anyone who served in Kandahar in the spring and summer of 2006), may seem a bit of an oxymoron. Arguably no branch of the Canadian Forces (CF) suffered more than logistics during what former Chief of Defence Staff General Rick Hillier used to call "the decade of darkness," when slashing budgets and numbers were the order of the day. Certainly, no other arm of the forces went so unappreciated, even by those who ought to have known better.

And no other group was so seriously undervalued for so long and then called upon to do so much when the CF returned to all-out combat that summer.

Just how unique was that particular tour in Afghanistan is still not very well understood by many back home.

To many Canadians, the war in Afghanistan seems all of a piece, one summer pretty much indistinguishable from another — there are always deaths, sombre ramp ceremonies, shots of soldiers sweating in that barren moonscape.

But the summer of 2006 *was* different.

As some elements of the battle group led by the 1st Battalion, Princess Patricia's Canadian Light Infantry, were in close-quarter gunfights every day, others were daily travelling hundreds of kilometres over bomb-laden roads (I use the term loosely) to keep them supplied with bullets, water, and rations, while back at Kandahar Air Field, still others worked 10-hour shifts in the sweltering heat of unglamorous tented workshops to keep the machinery humming.

As John told me once, the light armoured vehicles and others that logged two million old-fashioned miles that tour on Afghanistan's rutted river wadis and rugged ground were going through axles and differentials like popcorn.

Where now Canadian troops stick largely to the fertile areas west of Kandahar City, in those days they also moved to the farthest-flung parts of Kandahar Province, their own area of operations; several times rode to the rescue of the British in nearby Helmand Province; and oversaw the safe movement of Dutch soldiers into Uruzgan Province.

It was an astonishing demonstration of Canadian competence and resolve, and none of it would have been possible without the National Support Element (NSE), the small unit John commanded.

It was these men and women who kept what John calls the mobile Canadian Tire store on the road, and did it with far less armour and protection than their heavily armed peers in the infantry.

I remember a story Lieutenant-Colonel Ian Hope, the battle group commander, once told me. An infantry officer who was escorting in a resupply convoy complained about the man's sloppy driving. Lieutenant-Colonel Hope went over to the NSE sergeant in charge and asked how long they'd been on the road.

Four days, he replied.

Ian Hope was gobsmacked. As he said, "I realized just to what extent John [Conrad] was driving his people to keep us supplied."

John's book is about those unsung men and women who lived up to the ancient motto of soldiers who maintain supply lines and the tools of warfighting. It's *Arte et Marte*, Latin for "by skill and by fighting." In the summer of 2006, they proved they could do both. They did it without complaint — to be fair, they didn't have time to complain — and mostly unnoticed.

This book rectifies that. And because it's written by John Conrad, a soldier-poet, it does so beautifully.

ACKNOWLEDGEMENTS

A reconstruction of this magnitude can't be rendered without a number of willing deckhands. At the risk of offending anyone who helped me along, I would like to acknowledge the pivotal assistance I received from the following people who were close to the manuscript from its earliest beginnings.

I want to thank Christie Blatchford not only for her friendship and encouragement (both of which I value immeasurably) but also for the level of attention she focused upon logistics soldiers serving in the Canadian Forces. Her insightful descriptions of Canadian logistics in Kandahar were unique in my experience and important, for where Christie's pen goes, so too do many insightful, thoughtful Canadians.

I would like to thank Dr. Howard Coombs and Lieutenant-Colonel Rob McIlroy. I am indebted to Howard for his early review of the book's first three chapters and his outstanding suggestions. Rob McIlroy's innumerable reviews of the manuscript and his constant blend of criticism and encouragement were key in keeping my nose to the grindstone.

I would like to acknowledge the gracious assistance of Major Scott McKenzie, who contributed excerpts from his personal Kandahar diary, which he called "Afghanistan Updates," and Chief Warrant Officer Patrick Earles, who was a constant source of encouragement and advice. I can't imagine two men I would rather have at my side when the chips are down. Thank you both for your support and generosity throughout the writing of this book. I hope I have held the light high enough over our story.

Colonel Bernd Horn has been a source of inspiration, advice, and mentorship. He helped me frame a labyrinth of raw recollection and impressions into what I hope is an account that is readable for professional and civilian audiences alike. Any lapses into acronym and boring technobabble are my fault and not Bernd's. Thanks very much, Bernd, for believing in my unit and my book.

Finally, I must acknowledge my wife, Martha Rutherford Conrad, who has always waited so patiently for me to come home and has suffered through countless editorial reviews of the manuscript with the same courage and tenacity she brought to a convoy gone wrong. Thanks, Martha, you know full well that this story would not exist without you.

... and I heard, as it were the noise of thunder, one of the four beasts saying, Come and see. And I saw ... And when he had opened the fourth seal I heard the voice of the fourth beast say, Come and see. And I looked, and behold a pale horse: and his name that sat on him was Death and Hell followed with him.

— Book of Revelation

PREFACE

I will never forget the electric sense of shared enterprise between Lieutenant-Colonel Ian Hope and myself as we returned to Afghanistan in October 2005 to begin the final preparations for the mission in Kandahar. Were we really going to be taking our units, Canadian battalions, into a war? It seemed impossible and yet the handover briefings from our American counterparts kept bringing us back to the inevitable truth. You could see this on every line of every one of their faces. It is dangerous here.

— Lieutenant-Colonel John Conrad

I am a sucker for history, so there was no way in hell I was going to miss the briefing, overcrowded though it was. The Canadians were coming, and by God, we had a plan. The U.S. 173rd Airborne Brigade commander's austere plywood briefing room at the Kandahar Airfield (KAF) was chockablock in the late afternoon of 30 October 2005, but I pushed my way in and grabbed one of the remaining fringe seats at the back. Under the detailed International Security Assistance Force (ISAF) Stage 3 transition, the North Atlantic Treaty Organization (NATO) was expanding its jurisdiction to relieve the United States and Operation Enduring Freedom of singular responsibility for the volatile south of Afghanistan. Canada was to form the leading edge of the Stage 3 transition. The Canadian tactical reconnaissance team, led by Brigadier-General David Fraser, was just assembling to brief the in-place brigade commander when I slipped in. We were replacing the U.S. 173rd Airborne Brigade headquarters in southern Afghanistan and one of the brigade's battle groups in March 2006. Forces from the United Kingdom and the Netherlands would round out the rest of our Canadian-led Multinational Brigade. The brief was to give the 173rd Airborne, U.S. Task Force Bayonet, an idea about how the Canadian-led Multinational Brigade would gradually assume the reins in Regional Command South (RC South) the following March, some four months away.

The concept brief is an important cog in the process known as a "relief in place" where one fighting unit replaces another in the line. Key to the military definition of a relief in place is the presence of an active enemy. From the picture our U.S. counterparts had been painting for us all week, there would be plenty of that ingredient. Insurgent attacks on the Americans had been increasing throughout most of 2005. The 173rd Airborne was commanded by Colonel Kevin Owens, a tough paratrooper and talented officer with a knack for the intricacies of his mission. Earlier in the week I had been impressed by his ability to discuss the complex nuances of relationships at a municipal level between police chiefs, district commanders, and the various governors who operated in RC South. The articulate depth of his insight would have shattered the stereotype so many carry about the "Ugly American." There was no doubt in my mind that Owens commanded RC South with a surgeon's scalpel the way Theodore Roosevelt had carried a big stick. Colonel Owens, a "sky soldier," also had a solid appreciation for logistics. This appreciation was about to be demonstrated in spades.

The entire Canadian team had worked most of the day under canvas on the dust-pounded airfield preparing a heap of PowerPoint slides for the concept brief. I worked with Major Paul MacDonald, Brigadier-General Dave Fraser's brigade G4 (principal logistics staff officer) on the logistics part of the presentation. There were a number of complicated logistic wrinkles to be smoothed ranging in scale from how Canada would be allowed to award a contract for gravel, right up to full ownership of the sprawling airfield base itself. We pared back the logistics points to two sparse slides outlining only the big ticket items, the subjects I felt absolutely had to be addressed. However, during the final preparation for the presentation, the slides dealing with logistics were axed by a Canadian staff major in an effort to keep the brief at a reasonable length. General Fraser's presentation was indeed comprehensive save for one glaring area. Upon completion of his presentation, the general turned to Colonel Owens and asked the wiry commander of Task Force Bayonet if he had any further questions.

"Yeah ... Dave," Owens said. "What about logistics?"

Fraser blinked, clearly not expecting a salvo from this particular quarter. "Well ..." The general twisted in his chair and swept the rear of the conference room with his eyes.

"What's the plan?" Owens prompted. The commander of U.S. Task Force Bayonet seemed startled that the subject of logistics responsibilities on the forthcoming handover hadn't come up. At the very least the Americans were desperate to have someone share the financial burden of an expensive Kandahar Airfield. Undoubtedly Owens had been straining to hear some shred of information in this regard. In the silence that followed his question, the droning of an underachieving air conditioner filled the conference room. Sitting at the back, I felt that I could have hugged him. The difference between our army's professional culture and that of the war-weary United States was never so apparent.

"What about logistics?"

I am a logistics officer. I commanded the first Canadian combat logistics battalion into Kandahar in 2006, the men and women charged with the responsibility for moving the resupply convoys over a dangerous new sort of battlefield. My specific role in all of this was to shape the Canadian Task Force logistics structure on this landmark mission into southern Afghanistan. My battalion, with its bland and non-sexy title of National Support Element (NSE), deployed to Afghanistan in February 2006 after nearly 40 years of intellectual neglect of combat logistics by the Canadian Forces. As it would turn out, sustaining Canada's Task Force Orion in southern Afghanistan in 2006 would be a very near run thing: a brush with failure that was all too close. The logistic success of the Canadian battle group, Task Force Orion in 2006 constituted a remarkable military accomplishment and a nearly unbelievable story. With the noted exceptions of Christie Blatchford's despatches for the *Globe and Mail* and her bestselling book *Fifteen Days:*

Stories of Friendship, Life, and Death from Inside the New Canadian Army, and Rosie DiManno's stories in the *Toronto Star*, the logistic aspects of this story haven't attracted the attention of historians and journalists. To be blunt, a story like this would be hard-pressed to find a sponsor because it is a tale about logistics desperation. With few exceptions Canadian military history has ignored the combat logistics side of the battle — the nine-tenths of activity and effort that lie below the surface of all military operations. In my admittedly modest academic experience, I have noticed that the records at the National Defence Directorate of History and Heritage and Archives Canada are full of material on combat units but extremely lean on logistics memories.

In Kandahar, a dramatically different type of fight than Juno Beach, important visitors and members of the press again wanted to be at "the front" and near the thick of the fighting. Senior VIPs of the government and the Canadian Forces flew to the various forward operating bases by helicopter. This is the safest and most sensible way to move about in southern Afghanistan, but it cheats these leaders of the opportunity to experience the weight and smell of the humdrum logistic war on Afghanistan's roads. Many of the press stood among our convoy trucks beyond the wire as if they were in a copse of thick dark trees. They implored us to drive them to the forest, not initially appreciating that a large part of the story is here, not realizing at first that the enemy is everywhere and nowhere in particular. Insurgents attack where and when they choose, and the story that should be ringing loud through the modems of the press is that the new battlefield is an illusive, placid vista that could pass for a postcard picture, while combat logistics is more vital than ever to the success of the army on this new sort of battlefield.

I have read that during the intense fighting in the First World War the artillery barrages that came before major assaults on the Western Front sounded like thunder. The sound of this man-made thunder could be heard as far away as Paris and even in London, across the English Channel, in singular cases. The awful realities of combat were only experienced when one got close to the thunder. The farther a soldier was removed from the front, the less loud it became. In Kandahar the front-line is not so pronounced that it can be identified and fixed by anything as declarative as direction. And yet the sound of thunder is omnipresent. Combat can and does occur anywhere.

Logistics in Kandahar during Canada's return to sustained combat in 2006 owed its success to innumerable unsung heroes, the soldiers of all the various logistic and medical trades of the Canadian Forces. They served in a unit that was a bit too small to do its original support task in southern Afghanistan, and then was stretched as the Canadian infantry battle group found itself badly needed all over RC South, moving ever farther away from Kandahar Air Field, the main logistics hub, for increased periods of time.

A large part of my desire to write this book stemmed from a deep need to give voice to this exceptional group of men and women who rarely find a champion. I have grown up with these soldiers in the army and I have seen what they can achieve in peace and in war. They are ordinary people who do extraordinary things. I want people to understand the inside horrors and tribulations of doing this mundane replenishment work in southern Afghanistan.

The intent in these pages is to furnish a recollection as honest as I could capture it, complete with emotions, impressions, failures, and successes. The ensuing chapters offer neither an academic treatment of the Canadian campaign in Afghanistan nor a particularly detailed survey of logistics history. There are several such books available now that deal with Canada's role in Afghanistan. These books are not of uniform quality, but as a body of work they treat the strategic sinews of the campaign far better than I could attempt.

I will offer a brief overview of Canada's Afghanistan campaign and the logistics history of the Canadian Army only in as much detail as necessary to provide some context to the combat logistics challenges my unit faced on our country's return to Kandahar in a clear combat role. The unit you are about to meet in these pages numbered fewer than 300. They are the finest Canadians I have had the pleasure to know. Mothers, fathers, husbands, wives, sons and daughters, brothers, beer drinkers, hockey players, and NASCAR fans all of whom wore the maple leaf on their shoulders.

This is a war story of a logistics battalion, and in that respect, it is a highly unusual book. In our time, in our tiny Canadian Forces, logistics books are simply not written, yet, ironically, this is the exact time in the history of Canadian arms when they are needed the most.

I want to share with you at least a little of what the thunder said.

JOHN CONRAD
ORONO, ONTARIO, 2007

PART

1

1

This Side of Paradise

You have never seen a starry night sky until you have lifted your eyes to the heavens in northern Kandahar Province. I lay down to catch 40 winks on the wooden deck of the Arnes trailer in FOB [Forward Operating Base] Martello and was startled at the radiance and closeness of the stars all around me. I swear I could reach out and grab a handful of them. I felt I was peering into the very soul of God. We had avoided two IED attempts on our convoy up here on the endless day that was yesterday. Now set to return to KAF in less than an hour, I prayed I would not get any closer to my maker than I was right now, at least not today ...

— Lieutenant-Colonel John Conrad,
Kandahar Diary, April 2006

Warrant Officer Paul MacKinnon and Master Corporal Shawn Crowder of the National Support Element, Task Force Afghanistan's combat logistics battalion will tell you today that it was just an ordinary sojourn in hell, a typical convoy on this strange new sort of battlefield, but 15 May 2006 became one of those marrow-sucking Kandahar days that hits a snag and then gets progressively longer. MacKinnon and Crowder were on the precarious resupply convoy to the Gumbad safe house in northern Kandahar Province when smoke began to pour out of the engine of their Bison armoured vehicle. The Bison had broken down and the convoy was split in two, with some vehicles continuing the mission so that the outpost could be resupplied. MacKinnon, Crowder, and the rest of the troops and journalists that made up this convoy fragment settled in for a dreaded long halt. The term *long halt* is brimming with memories and meaning for Canadian soldiers familiar with Afghanistan. It means you must wait for heavier recovery assistance; you can't press on. The long halt recalls endless hours at the top of the world when you scrutinize the peerless blue sky of Afghanistan and watch dust devils weave their eerie paths across the broken land. A millennium can pass in an hour. A soldier on a long halt stares up at infinity while contemplating the potential horrors of the immediate. For Paul MacKinnon and Shawn Crowder a thousand years of waiting was beginning.

Gumbad is a lonely infantry platoon outpost jammed in the heart of Taliban-dominated territory. Our tour of duty was two and a half months old on 15 May and already trips to Gumbad were met with gritted teeth. Over 100 kilometres northwest of the main coalition base at KAF, the patrol house at Gumbad can only be reached using a combination of barely discernable secondary roads, dried-out riverbeds called wadis, and flat-out, cross-country driving. No matter how one looks at it there are only two meagre roads in to the patrol house — two paths offering the enemy the advantage of predictability. The spread of terrain around the patrol house is disarmingly beautiful, reminiscent of Alberta's badlands or the raw spread of land along the Dempster Highway in Canada's Far North. Here in northern Kandahar, however, the landscape is rife with jury-rigged munitions that can abruptly sweep away your life.

These munitions come in all shapes and sizes and are made from the most rudimentary components and are called improvised explosive devices (IEDs). It is positively eerie how basic and simply constructed many of these IEDs are. Insurgents make full use of these crudely rendered weapons and plant them like macabre crop seed on Afghanistan's roads, culverts, and riverbeds. IEDs are the preferred weapon of the enemy for use against Canadian convoys. It was near Gumbad that one such explosive device consisting of two pairs of double-stacked anti-tank mines claimed the lives of four Canadian soldiers three weeks back on 22 April 2006.

The Canadian battle group was doggedly holding the Gumbad outpost, waiting for the arrival of Afghan authorities to share and ultimately relieve them of the task. In the meantime the job hung like an albatross around the neck of 1 Platoon, Alpha Company, 1st Battalion, Princess Patricia's Canadian Light Infantry (1 PPCLI). The gritty Canadian infantry platoon had to be sustained by lumbering logistics trucks escorted in under the muzzles of LAV III fighting vehicles. It was murder, literally, getting up to Gumbad, and the Canadians ended up holding the rustic outpost until the end of June 2006.

Alexander the Great reputedly camped along the shores of Lake Arghandab with an army of 30,000 Greek soldiers. Today the turquoise lake stands out like a precious jewel in the stark landscape along the Tarin Kot Highway. All Canadian convoys going to the northern portion of the province — either the Gumbad Patrol House or Forward Operating Base Martello — must pass this lake.

Warrant Officer MacKinnon and Master Corporal Crowder weren't looking at Gumbad on 15 May. You feel an IED detonation for several nanoseconds before you actually hear it. They were just settling into the defensive posture of a long halt around their disabled Bison vehicle, beginning the wait for recovery when the shock waves and subsequent noise of an enormous explosion reached them from farther up the wadi. One of the newest vehicles in the Canadian fleet, a mine-resistant RG 31 or Nyala, in the small convoy that pressed on, had struck an IED device and blown apart. The fickle hand of fate had kept the NSE soldiers out of the blast area. Had MacKinnon and Crowder not broken down they would have been the next vehicle back from the Nyala. Fortunately there were no immediate fatalities in the strike, but the wounds of the soldiers were serious.

The race against time for successful medical evacuation had begun. The problem now was that the limited recovery assets from KAF suddenly had a higher priority vehicle casualty to deal with. Back on the airfield, 100 kilometres to the south, smart operations staffs were working on stretching limited resources to get both vehicles out. MacKinnon smoked a cheap cigar as he watched the hours evaporate in the blistering 45 degree Celsius heat. He was normally part of the NSE operations team, the resilient staff that worked on problems exactly like this from KAF in tandem with the 1 PPCLI Infantry Battle Group, and he knew that whatever solution was hammered out at the enormous coalition base wouldn't assist them anytime soon.

Another eternity had passed by the time Paul MacKinnon noted the arrival of several Afghan locals. He took his interpreter over to talk with them. They told him that they were farmers. The Afghans went on to explain that between 20 and 30 more men would be joining them from a nearby village to sleep in their fields tonight. Time stood still between two beats of MacKinnon's heart. This wasn't right. A streetwise Cape Breton boy, Paul MacKinnon had heard enough. He realized that the time had come for them to help themselves.

"They're gathering," he told Bob Weber, one of the Canadian reporters travelling with them. "They're the wrong age and the wrong attitude." A battlefield mechanic by trade, MacKinnon had already mapped out a rudimentary withdrawal plan in his mind in the space between his conversation with the Afghan farmer and his return to the vehicles. The goddamn Bison would be moving whether it wanted to or not. He pulled aside one of the sergeants and laid out a new course. "Sarge, we're not staying here…."

The Canadians cabled their stricken Bison to a healthy one that had stayed with them for security reinforcement and loaded up the collection of Canadian reporters who had been toughing out the day with them. Master Corporal Crowder returned to the driver compartment and began steering the dead Bison without the benefit of power. Manually steering an armoured vehicle across Kandahar Province is a brutally physical task. Over the next 12 hours the small convoy laboured to cover the 100 kilometres back to KAF. They finally arrived back at the base in the wee hours before dawn exhausted and spent. MacKinnon described the outcome as one of the very best given the situation they had faced over the past 20 hours. Nobody died. In fact, it would be two more days before another Canadian soldier was killed in Kandahar.

Paul MacKinnon woke up later that day to discover that his greater concern was with his wife. MacKinnon was an ex-smoker who had long fought the itch to start up again. His wife, checking the day's news on the Internet back in Edmonton, had just seen a photo that showed him smoking a huge stogie on the deck of his Bison armoured vehicle, looking all the world like the Canuck version of Sergeant Rock. Shawn Crowder woke up to find his arms on fire with pain. His limbs were purple with bruises from steering the stricken Bison back from the nether regions of the province without power steering. He dismissed any inquiries into his health with a disgusted shake of the head.

"When are we heading out again, sir?" This was the only remark he made. Discussion of yesterday was firmly closed. This was the battlefield of our generation and it didn't care if you were a politician, a journalist or a soldier. It wouldn't discern what cap badge or rank you wore.

> I remember that when I came to KAF in January the outgoing guys were building a new monument that included pieces of the one we had in Kabul. The centrepiece was a large rock that was found near where Sergeant Short and Corporal Beerenfenger were killed around Kabul in 2003, and attached to it were plaques bearing the names of soldiers killed to date. The rock was pretty much covered and I remember thinking I hope we don't fill up all the extra space with our soldiers' names. We are now building a new, bigger monument.
>
> — Major Scott McKenzie, "Afghanistan Updates"

In early August 2006 I made a point of going to the fortress-like building known as the Taliban Last Stand or TLS. TLS wouldn't have looked out of place as a set for the canteen on planet Tatooine in George Lucas's *Star Wars* films. The building is surrounded by the incessant roar of transport aircraft and choppers that feed and feed from the giant air base. Possessed of thick mud walls and prominent decorative arches alien to western architecture, TLS serves now as a multipurpose administration facility and the KAF Air Movements Terminal.[1] It was supposedly the building that held the last Taliban resistance during the early invasion of Afghanistan in 2002 — Operation Enduring Freedom's first year. As the story goes, a JDAMs missile from the U.S. Air Force ended the "last stand" with pinpoint lethality.

A joint NSE-1 PPCLI convoy makes its way north on the Tarin Kot Highway from KAF to begin work on Forward Operating Base Martello in early April 2006. FOB Martello eventually served as a patrol platform for Alpha Company and as a much-needed way station for Dutch forces making their way to Tarin Kot out of KAF.

Our relief in place, the term the military uses for being replaced while in contact with an enemy, was in full swing with the new NSE of the Royal Canadian Regiment's 1st Battalion. The rotation flights home had started two weeks earlier with C-130 Hercules aircraft bringing fresh faces in the morning and ushering out bits and pieces of my unit in the afternoon. Today was the day that Sergeant Pat Jones, a professional army driver and convoy leader in my NSE, would depart KAF to begin his journey home. I had to see him off.

"Well, Jonesy, you made it," I muttered as I patted this stalwart soldier on the back. There are no words to describe how difficult it was to see Sergeant Jones leave. But he had to. He was utterly used up, charred black on the inside.

"Yup" was all Jones could muster. He seemed surprised that I might notice his imminent departure and perplexed that I had made the effort to see him off. To that minute he never had so much as an inkling how much psychological momentum he had given to his commanding officer.

"How are you feeling?"

"Fine, sir. Fine ... just ... tired of seeing dead people."

It was the last time I ever spoke to him.

The battlefield of the logistics soldier lies so heavily entrenched in the realm of the mind — the psychological plane. Unlike our brothers in the combat arms we rarely go on the offensive. There is no cathartic release for the logistician that an attack can permit the infantryman. The logistic soldier in Kandahar rides with passive optimism that he or she will come up swinging after the attack. But whether you live or die, whether you get to come up fighting, depends not on your physical fitness, your intellect, or your prowess with the rifle. Instead your survival hangs on such random factors as vehicle armour, proximity to the blast, and pure luck. Providence. That is hard to accept. The first move in a convoy fight belongs to the enemy and that is terrifically unsettling. Soon every Toyota that strays too close to your truck resembles a bomb, every colourful kite is a semaphore signal, and every smile from an Afghan pedestrian betrays a sinister secret. Ground convoys extract a continuous toll on the psychological reserves of a logistics unit.

We nearly lost Sergeant Pat Jones on the first week of the tour. On 3 March 2006, two days after the Canadians took the reins from the American Task Force Gun Devil and their supporting Logistics Task Force 173 in Kandahar Province, one of our convoys was attacked.

The convoy was using Highway 1 to deliver supplies and personnel to their new assignments with the Canadian Provincial Reconstruction team at Camp Nathan Smith, in Kandahar City. Ironically there was a military investigation team from Canada onboard conducting an investigation into the death of Mr. Glynn Berry from the Department of Foreign Affairs who had been killed in a convoy the month before we had arrived. Two of the passengers in Ian Hope's LAV III were from my supply staff, Master Warrant Officer Mitch Goudreau and Sergeant Bird. Bird was a reservist, a part-timer, from the East Coast who was destined to become the main supply purchasing agent for Camp Nathan Smith. Mitch Goudreau was a well-travelled figure inside the PPCLI having come to the NSE from the magnificent 2nd Battalion in Shilo, Manitoba. Goudreau was along to see his subordinate properly introduced and installed at the camp. Two kilometres east of the city, their LAV III was attacked by a vehicle-borne suicide bomber. The vehicle had six rounds of artillery ammunition onboard when it detonated beside the LAV. In the ensuing blast the crew commander, Master Corporal Loewen, was badly hurt. Loewen's arm was nearly completely severed and his life was in immediate peril. The Bison armoured vehicle in the column pulled up beside the LAV III and began to assist with medical triage. Sergeant Pat Jones was the vehicle crew commander.[2] Jones witnessed the entire blast from his perch behind the Bison's C6 machine gun and he followed his drills to serve as a medical evacuation platform for the LAV III casualties. A combination of Bison passengers, 1 PPCLI, and NSE soldiers provided immediate first aid to Master Corporal Loewen. Because of the proximity of KAF, the convoy commander decided to evacuate him by ground in Jones's armoured vehicle instead of asking for air evacuation. Time in a medical evacuation is the critical factor. A handful of minutes can make the difference between life and death. Jones pushed his old Bison so hard in the urgency to get Loewen back to KAF that the vehicle's engine burst into flames. Just a few metres shy of the main gate into the camp, smoke began to stream from the vehicle's engine. Power evaporated from the machine and it came to an abrupt stop, maddeningly on the very doorstep of KAF.

What followed over the next few minutes is best described as barely managed chaos. Similar scenes have been played out by scores of Canadian soldiers in Afghanistan since 2006. Priority one was the badly injured Loewen who needed to keep moving forward to medical attention. Every second of delay deepened the need. As the Bison burned, the rear exit ramp jammed tight in the closed position, trapping its passengers. The top hatch of the vehicle, known lovingly as the family hatch, had to be forced open manually and Loewen was passed through and cross-loaded onto a the roof of another vehicle in the convoy, a Canadian Mercedes G-Wagon. As he was fastened securely to a stretcher, a couple of quick-thinking soldiers stood in the doors of the truck and held the stretcher firmly in place while they careened through the gate into KAF and finished the race to the Role 3 military hospital.

With Loewen again on his way, Sergeant Jones sorted through his remaining priorities and turned his attention onto the Bison driver. Corporal "Killer" Mackinnon, a military truck driver serving on his first ever tour of duty, was stuck in the driver's compartment with eyes as wide as pie plates. He was suffering badly from the heat of the burning engine in the neighbouring cowling.

"Killer, hang in there!" was all Jones grunted as he climbed back on top of the vehicle to assist his driver. Jones pulled up hard on the back of MacKinnon's body armour. I recall hearing about a farmer near our home in the mid-1970s who had lifted a corn harvesting wagon off of his daughter's crushed legs in order to save her life. The adrenaline-inspired moment always harboured elements of the unbelievable in my mind until what Jones did. Lifting a man vertically out of a driver compartment is a Herculean task on a good day but Pat Jones succeeded in freeing MacKinnon on one of the worst days of his life. Although Killer MacKinnon was scared shitless, the only physical damage he suffered was minor burns and a melted pistol holster. As he turned to his next task, Jones wasn't as lucky. The vehicle had a halon fire extinguisher system that is supposed to allow for external detonation. On this day of days the external release didn't work. Tripping the extinguisher could only be done from inside the machine, and without so much as a "here I go!" Pat Jones re-entered the burning armoured vehicle. In the process of executing this drill and releasing the extinguishing chemical he received a lung full of halon. It would be days before he could stop coughing and hacking.

When Paddy Earles and I visited Sergeant Pat Jones later on the night of 3 March in the military hospital, I got my first real glimpse of the effects of war. Master Corporal Loewen lay bandaged and sedated across the ward. Pat Jones was sequestered inside a semi-private enclosure beside a young captain with appendicitis. He was sitting up as we came in, but something was tangibly wrong.

Pat Jones was a bear of a man. He routinely took his furlough from the army late in the year and derived great enjoyment from his annual hunting expeditions in northern Alberta. Jonesy had served as a young corporal with me when I was a company commander in Edmonton. During the workup training for Kandahar, he had been a rock of stability, a fine senior non-commissioned officer (NCO) and one of only a handful of convoy commanders we had to rely upon.

The look in his eyes that night at the KAF hospital was alien to the man I knew so well. He was careful, I thought, too careful to say all the right things. We could tell that he was unsettled, struggling hard against things unseen. The change in him shook my confidence. Every commanding officer, every leader, cultivates his core team, his "go to" men and women who can be trusted to get the job done when the going is difficult. Sergeant Pat Jones was born to be one of these men, and replacing an NCO of his calibre was next to impossible. Standing in the plywood Golgotha of the Role 3 hospital, I had my first bout of anxiety over the small size of the NSE. This was the third day of our mission. I had really screwed up.

Although I knew before we deployed that I didn't have enough support soldiers, the fact that I might not have brought enough convoy leaders to see us through this mission never dawned on me. These sergeants are like bishops on a chessboard. They are gritty, experienced, and worth their weight in gold. Paddy Earles and I left the hospital and went for coffee at the little Canadian Exchange café behind our sea container headquarters. I was in hell that night, frightened on a host of different levels. If we could lose a man like Jones from our logistics team on day three of the mission, what would the next six and a half months bring?

We didn't lose him. His lungs cleared of halon, and the faraway look in his eyes ebbed. If the haunting new tone in his voice didn't completely go away, it at least waned to a point where it could no longer be easily detected and he returned to duty later that same week. General Rick Hillier presented Jones with a Chief of the Defence Staff Coin, followed later by the commendation, for his actions on 3 March 2006. What Jones probably didn't know was that by his courage both beyond the wire and inside the KAF Role 3 hospital, he had restored my confidence. I was, after all, a rookie to real war. The NSE had been tested, our soldiers had been hurt, and we were dusted off and back to work the next day. For reasons that even to this day I don't understand, this incident was pivotal. It galvanized me for the darker storms yet to come.

> We got your phone message. We hope to leave it on the machine till you're back. Your dad and I love you and pray for your safe return.
> — First Letter from My Parents, 10 February 2006

2

Children of a Lesser God

If you are reading this it means for sure that I am not coming home ... I am so sorry. I do not know for certain how I have been killed but I have a pretty good idea ... When you tell people about me please don't stress the fact that I was sitting on my ass inside a truck with my rifle between my knees when I died. Tell the kids, tell my parents ... that I died with my face toward the enemy ...
— Lieutenant-Colonel John Conrad,
"Just in Case Letter," Kandahar Airfield, 2006

WHAT ABOUT LOGISTICS?

I have to believe that outside of the Canadian Forces it cannot be so shameful to be a logistics or a supply chain employee in a successful company. Working in corporate logistics, like being part of the prestigious German general staff, connotes a certain level of prestige. And for a good reason. Logistics in the corporate world is a big part of any company's bottom line and it requires talent and experience. Chances are that you yourself have had to dabble in logistics at one time or another. Consider the popular television commercial that says that a family of four will consume three tons in groceries each year. If you are a farmer, business person, or just a time-impoverished parent who has had to balance hockey practice pickups with grocery runs, you've worked on a logistics problem.

The word *logistics* comes from the Greek *logos*, with a contemporary breadth of meaning that covers ratio, word, calculation, reason, speech, and oration.[3] In other words, logistics was related to the whole spectrum of thinking and reasoning as the ancient Greeks perceived it and its growth as a discipline came out of the need for the armies of antiquity to support themselves as they moved forward from city states to campaigns. To that end, being involved in logistics is like being harnessed to the brains of your organization. NATO has defined logistics as the science of planning and carrying out the movement and maintenance of forces. For my 24 years in the regular army this clean definition is the one that served us. I think the NATO definition is somewhat two-dimensional and intellectually canalizing. It does not even begin to hint at the myriad trials and friction that bedevils a combat service support plan. After a career of supporting Canadian land forces in three different continents in classic peacekeeping operations and in war, I challenge whether logistics, at its core, is a science at all. Logistics is the discipline that deals with the provision of goods and services to an institution, but what I believe more than ever after Kandahar is that the psychological aspects prevail and in that respect, logistics is far more about art than science. The most important facets of logistics in war reside in the kingdom of the mind. At its best, logistics is the well-planned, logical offspring of a fertile imagination harnessed early to the demands of the tactical plan. At its worst, logistics is a crudely rendered afterthought stapled to a military disaster.

The Canadian brand of military logistics or combat service support grew up, from Confederation forward, with a young army that recognized its worth and absolute necessity. Canadian soldiers insisted upon home-grown logistics; they demanded their own. Logistics was once a valued component inside our field force, a necessary partner in the Canadian manner of fighting. It was initially homespun and somewhat crudely strung together to support the large militia operation in Western Canada in 1885. Logistics was purchased from Great Britain in South Africa, in 1900, during the Boer War — the first war to showcase Canadian troops beyond our borders. During the Boer War, Canadian troops longed for their own dedicated logistics support. They grew to resent the "country cousin" treatment they received from the British army logistics system. By the time Europe plunged into the First World War, Canada had its own logistics units. In many ways the last segment of that war witnessed the zenith of Canadian Army logistics achievement — to the point where Canadian logistics units were the envy of the Allied Forces in France. The senior leadership in the British Expeditionary Force (BEF) and its superb Canadian component, the Canadian Corps, was able to overcome a contemporary institutional bias that encouraged commanders to remain aloof from the logistics and administrative staffs.[4] The attention afforded logistics in 1916 by Field Marshal Haig, the commander of the BEF, and Lieutenant-General Byng, Haig's subordinate and the commander of the Canadian Corps, was instrumental in overcoming the challenges of the new, industrialized battlefield and attaining offensive success in late summer 1918. In the Second World War, Canada again maintained logistics systems up to and including sophisticated corps level units. The Canadian Army, in keeping with its allies, had gone to great lengths to mechanize support units, ensuring that replenishment and repairs could be organized and provided quickly to its fighting divisions in Italy and northwest Europe. Finally, the Korean War saw small Canadian logistics units achieve great results serving inside a Commonwealth division in direct support to 25 Canadian Infantry Brigade. But for a variety of reasons, consideration for matters logistic in the tiny Canadian Army between the Korean War (1950–53) and a series of gut-wrenching convoy assaults north of Pashmul, Afghanistan, in 2006 has been negligible.

Years of disinterest in logistics training and development in the lean years after the Korean War and particularly after dramatic reorganization of logistics as part of unification in 1968 have left Canada's army with only one true logistics asset — the men and women in the various trades who make up the rank and file. The proud corps histories of the various logistics services were wiped away under unification of the three services. Combat logistics soldiers no longer enjoy even the soothing balm that a regimental family affords. Regiments like the storied Van Doos, the Royal Canadian Regiment, and the Princess Patricia's Canadian Light Infantry have these families and regimental associations and their members draw strength from them. Logistics soldiers are just not considered this way. Why not? Our soldiers possess a marked resourcefulness and a warrior ethos that is alarmingly incongruous with the valued bureaucratic principles of the Canadian Forces Logistics Branch. The combat logistics soldiers offer a capability well suited to the contemporary battlefield that is far out of proportion to the level of investment and interest demonstrated by the wider leadership of Canadian Forces. This lack of interest makes the Canadian Forces brittle as a fighting institution. Decades of cultural disinterest in combat logistics put my NSE in a precarious tactical position supporting Task Force Orion on a new sort of battlefield in 2006. Only the efforts of 300 remarkable Canadian soldiers carried the day.

An NSE convoy passes a group of Afghans as it shunts supplies north. Outside the complex congestion of Kandahar the threat to a convoy seemed to diminish. However, improvised explosive devices (IEDs) are often used in rural areas.

Inside the Canadian Forces and the army in particular there are strict and ancient pecking orders. In the army context, the holy triumvirate of the combat arms are at the top of a robust cap-badge hierarchy. The combat arms comprise the infantry, artillery, and armoured corps. The combat engineers come in next, having been granted combat arms status in 1993. Combat support arms like the intelligence and the signals corps are found on the next level down in the hierarchy, less prestigious than the combat arms but markedly ahead of the steerage class logistics soldier. At the base of this entire heap are the men and women of logistics services, what we call in military parlance the combat service support (CSS) professions. These soldiers are the medics, suppliers, transporters, mechanics, to cite a few — soldiers like mine. The elite of our military are indeed our combat arms units. This is the way it should always be. After all, you would not need logistics if there was no infantry section holding a ridge line somewhere on the lonely battlefield. At the same time, however, military logistics in the Canadian Forces is viewed as something less than merely non-elite. Military logistics in Canada is viewed with near disdain.

In 2006 what turned this hierarchical pyramid on its ear was the nature of the fight in Kandahar Province. Karl von Clausewitz, the esteemed German author and pre-eminent thinker on the subject of warfare, postulated that at the centre of war is fighting. On this new sort of battlefield all soldiers, regardless of rank, stature, or cap badge, have to be prepared to fight. Indeed mundane logistics convoys are among the most dangerous missions undertaken by Canadian men and women overseas. There are lessons to be shared from the Kandahar style of battlefield. The biggest of these from my perspective is that logistics has to become part of combat operations when there are no such words as *front* and *rear* anymore. The line between the combat arms and combat logistics soldiers on the modern battlefield has become blurred.

The battlefield upon which we find ourselves is dramatically altered from the ones understood by our grandfathers. The thunder of combat can erupt at anytime from any direction. An attack can occur in a city, town or open sandy road. In many respects the difficulty in moving *matériel* on the battlefield today is completely different from the logistics challenges that confronted General Byng, during what Canadian Army historian C.P. Stacey called Canada's "Hundred Days" of 1918, or what Field Marshal Bernard Montgomery dealt with in Normandy in 1944. What is clear above all else is that in the complex landscape of the contemporary operating environment, logistics must weigh more prominently in the army's thinking than it has over the past 40 years.

Canadian mortars stand ready for use at an artillery manoeuvre area (AMA). On average, routine resupply was conducted three to four times a week to sustain this gun position in northern Kandahar Province. The superb artillery support furnished by the new Canadian guns has re-established indirect fire as the queen of battle. Artillery was a lifesaver for Canadian and Afghan National Security Forces operating in RC South.

On this new sort of battlefield, plied by Canadian convoys, on any given day you may not get to where you are going and there is no guarantee that you will make it back to where you came from. Anywhere along the line between departure and destination you must be prepared to fight for your life. But despite this paramount reality the logistics community is still not as highly regarded as other parts of the army. The hierarchical cap-badge pyramid of the Canadian Army is alive and well here at home. Generations of officers have grown up with a healthy disinterest for logistics and there is no clear signal, even against the realities of Kandahar, that this cultural malaise will dissolve any time soon.

It was not always this way.

3

Storms of Our Grandfathers

General Arthur Currie, the brilliant commander of the Canadian
Corps, deliberately created a logistics crisis before the move to
Amiens from the Ypres Salient on 1 August 1918. Like a quarterback
looking to his right to freeze the defence, he suddenly turned left and
sent the large Canadian formation rumbling noiselessly south. Currie
did not inform his chief of logistics, General Farmar, about the move
until 29 July 1918, giving the logistics staff approximately 24 hours of
planning before the Corps had to start moving.[5]

The coming offensive down at Amiens was defined by a tight secrecy
at all levels of preparation. The presence of Canadians, who had come
to be used as shock troops inside the British Expeditionary Force, would
easily telegraph a coming offensive to the Germans. Transportation and
movement planning were mightily tested because of this requirement
for absolute secrecy. In the course of compressed preparation time, the
subordinate divisional logistics staffs were left with a mere five days of
advance notice. By 1 August 1918, when the Canadians began to move
down to the Amiens sector for the coming fight, there remained only
six days to extend the logistics conduit from Boulogne. Furthermore,
the Corps would need to move and prepare for battle in an unfamil-
iar sector under complicated conditions. It was assigned only two main
supply routes — the Amiens-Roye road and the Amiens-Villers Breton-
neux. These two roads could only be used at night, as recorded in the
Canadian War Diaries: "The Division is now in the first stage of a concentration march preparatory to assembling in battle positions. Surprise
is to be the essence of the operation and therefore, all movement is to

be restricted to the cover of darkness ... transport is to be parked under trees and troops not to be allowed to move about ..."[6]

To complicate matters, the Canadian sector in Amiens had been a French sector, bereft of the compatible logistics pieces to sustain a British formation.[7] This placement in a new, non-British sector meant that the logistics chain would have to haul from refilling points farther afield. There was no end to the administrative challenges in the preparatory actions for the Canadian Corps, but when the balloon went up at H hour on 8 August 1918, by God, the Canadians made it rain.

The accomplishments of the Canadian Corps throughout the Hundred Days campaign were plentiful. High among the list of achievements was a logistics proficiency that was the envy of the British Army in France.

When you enter Normandy Hall, the breeding ground of leadership at the Canadian Army's superb Command and Staff College in Kingston, the first thing that strikes the eye is an ancient oak ship's rudder mounted on the wall. A tiny brass plate next to the oak explains that it was recovered during the construction of Normandy Hall in 1953. As the story goes, the rudder belonged to a French warship that had been ransacked and burned during the ballsy raid on Fort Frontenac by Lieutenant-Colonel Bradstreet in July 1758. Bradstreet had launched the raid on the Fort Frontenac from Oswego, New York, with 2,737 men. It was a clever strategic move that knocked out the logistics base of the French, sending reverberating shock waves all the way down the Ohio Valley. The account of the raid conjures up a number of heroic images and vistas of audacity and triumph. For a combat logistician, this vignette brings other thoughts to mind.

July in Kingston is oppressively hot and muggy. This probably reduced Bradstreet's requirement for canvas, firewood, and baggage, but water, ammunition, and rations would be needed to sustain his men. Did the raiding party merely fill their canteens in the Cataraqui River? One assumes so. How many boats of ammunition did Bradstreet bring, what sorts of specialized equipment, and how much food did his force, almost as large as our current Canadian Task Force Afghanistan, require? How long did he intend to fight, presuming everything went well? These questions fall into the realm of logistics, and though they might occur to the disciplined student of history, they are usually among the last ones to be considered by Canadian officers. The logistics specialist can grasp the operational points of the Bradstreet raid, but he or she must reduce aspects of the plan to a time-honoured calculus. The application of violence, both blood and steel, must be appreciated in an additional dimension.

Canada and Afghanistan pose the same challenges to an army: crushing geography and a climate that can kill. In the earliest military history of our great nation, logistics were synonymous with survival. We live in a land defined by large tracts of space with a climate that can often be lethal to its inhabitants. Canada is the second-largest country in the world in terms of geographical area, comprising some 9,984,670 square kilometres and stretching for nearly 9,000 kilometres along the border it shares with the United States.[8] From the strategic support bases of Hochelaga and Stadacona in Quebec, through to the building of the great transcontinental railway, logistics systems have been designed to carry essential *matériel* across our vast and rugged country. The Red River Rebellion of 1869–70 showcased the earliest, rudimentary editions of these Canadian lines of supply. The Red River crisis was the first military test for the young Dominion of Canada and logistics in a Canadian context. The rebellion was sparked when the Dominion government purchased the belt of Rupert's Land from the Hudson's Bay Company. The less than 10,000 residents of what is now Manitoba were unhappy with the Dominion's plans, and under the leadership of Louis Riel stood up in resistance. Riel formed a provisional government in Manitoba in an act meant to show defiance and Métis sovereignty. A federal force of 1,044 men, made up of some 400 British regulars and enlisted Canadians from Ontario, was mobilized and placed under the leadership of General Garnet Wolseley. The Dominion force followed an arduous route across Lake Superior, and a "rugged canoe route" from the lakehead to Manitoba.[9] It can be said without exaggeration that getting to Manitoba was half of the battle. The Dominion forces were successful in quashing the Red River Rebellion without bloodshed. Riel fled in exile to Montana.

Louis Riel later incited the North-West Rebellion of 1885 in what is now known as Saskatchewan. This rebellion illustrates well the logistics challenges a big country like Canada poses to a fighting force. Riel set up a second provisional government at Batoche and enlisted the military leadership of Gabriel Dumont to fight the Dominion forces. The great transcontinental railway was not yet complete, but by using the existing Canadian Pacific Railway lines and American railways south of the border, an effective movement system was put in place. Of greater import was what Desmond Morton has called the "ready-made supply system" in the form of the network of Hudson's Bay posts to glean the bulk of the required supplies.[10] General Middleton had to lean on these hardy trading posts to furnish the supply needs of his force. Over the course of two western uprisings, the Canadian militia got the job done, even though it lacked dedicated military logistics.

The Boer War (1899–1902) saw a small Canadian Expeditionary Force made up of newly minted units such as the Royal Canadian Regiment and, in the second contingent, the Royal Canadian Dragoons. The Canadian detachment fought inside the larger framework of the British Army and received its logistics support from it. More than 8,000 Canadian soldiers fought in the Boer War, and yet there was no formal Canadian supply chain. The Canadian government was responsible to pay for the initial kitting of the Canadian contingent and the costs of their transport to theatre of operations. Once in South Africa, logistic support to the Canadians was the responsibility of the British Army. Two hard lessons were borne of Canadian experiences in the Boer War. The first lesson centred on the Canadian soldier's first look at an irregular style of warfare. After the British victory at Paardeburg, in which Canadian forces figured prominently, the Boers reverted to guerrilla-style tactics to further their aims. These tactics included attacking British supply lines on the veldt, which made resupply a tactical challenge. The second lesson followed from the tendency for Canadian troops to be served after the regular British units by the British Army logistics system. Victims of another nation's supply chain, it was not uncommon for Canadian soldiers to endure weeks on half rations or to be routinely served only after British units. This tier-two treatment left an indelible impression on the contingent and it cut a deep groove in the memory of the fledgling Canadian Army: it is always better to bring your own. When war erupted in Europe a decade later, the Canadian Expeditionary Force would at last include tactical logistics units among their number. We have been bringing our own logistics troops to Canada's fights ever since.

TRIUMPH OF PERSONALITIES

Most of us tend to think of the First World War as a mass of senseless bloodshed — an unfortunate clash of empires in which there are few relevant military lessons. It is easy to understand this view. The "Great War for Civilization" claimed over 60,000 Canadian lives out of a population of eight million.[11] A modest exhibit at the Canadian War Museum struck me most poignantly in the spring of 2007. This particular exhibit displayed the ephemera and awards a grieving mother received after her two sons were killed in action in the war. The two Memorial Crosses behind the glass mesmerized me. These little bits of silver were all that the grieving mother had to show for her brilliant boys, her best heart's blood. Losses like these were widespread across the Dominion of Canada and virtually every hamlet and village in Canada maintains some form of memorial tribute to their First World War fallen.[12] I have never contemplated the silver cross from the perspective of knowing so many fresh recipients.

Canadian General Dave Fraser, my boss in Kandahar and the commander of the Canadian Task Force as well as the Multinational Brigade in RC South, had to prepare his fighting force for a new type of battlefield. Such a difficult intellectual task was not without precedent. Combat in the trenches of Europe from 1914 to 1918 was defined by an industrialized lethality that rocked the paradigm of contemporary field commanders. The logistics structures and systems bearing the weight of the British Expeditionary Force and by extension the Canadian Corps on the Western Front were initially static and lacked the capacity to support this industrialized battlefield.[13] The British commanders that held direct sway over the Canadian Corps, specifically Douglas Haig and one of his subordinate corps's commanders, Julian Byng, invested time in their sustainment structure. Both of these generals were able to enhance the logistics functionality of the Canadian Corps in a profound manner. The British Army Field Service Regulations (Part 2) of 1912, which is like an owner's manual for operating in the army, encouraged commanders to remain aloof from matters of administration and logistics.[14] This is an antique bias that unfortunately still finds traction in the current edition of the Canadian Forces. Remarkably, the actions of Haig and Byng strongly suggest that they understood the importance of logistics in the projection of combat power despite the prevailing convention of their time.

Has history been unkind to Field Marshal Haig? Haig's reputation has been shredded for his steerage through such atrocious campaigns as the Somme and Third Ypres. Most military libraries hold at least some books and academic papers that criticize his blunders. I do not consider myself an apologist for Haig but I believe it is easy to overlook accomplishments that speak to his abilities and staying power as the commander-in-chief of the BEF from late 1915 through to the end of the war. Can you imagine for a second the moral and physical demands that such an immense responsibility would have placed on the man for such a long period? Gervais Phillips strikes an accurate chord in recollecting Haig's administrative accomplishments:

> His army was well supplied in the field, his wounded
> swiftly evacuated and well cared for ... the figure of Haig
> looms ever larger as that of the man who foresaw more
> accurately than most, who endured longer than most and
> who inspired most confidence amongst his fellows.[15]

Not only did Haig have to solve the challenges that came with unprecedented volumes of *matériel*, but he also had to deal with enormous advances in technology. Some of the biggest seeds of innovation that would impact the Canadian Corps during the Hundred Days were sown at his insistence after the butchery of the Somme offensive of 1916. Most prominently, Haig knew that reworking the entire logistics system was imperative. During the height of the battle, the replenishment system proved incapable of delivering the crushing volumes of *matériel* required at the front. A report of the Ministry of Overseas Military Forces of Canada recorded: "After the Battle of the Somme, it was clearly proven that road and animal transport could not alone bring forward ... the weight of war *matériel* required to stage a modern battle."[16]

Haig was able to overcome contemporary army disdain for all matters of logistics and administration. He had to. As he knew, and as we learned again and again in southern Afghanistan in 2006, there are rarely service publications and books to help you solve the seminal problem of the day. The problems of your generation tend to be off the known chart. Against strong military advice to the contrary, the commander of the BEF sought the assistance of a civilian transportation expert, Sir Eric Geddes to overhaul the sustainment system.[17]

Sir Eric Geddes took a basic, first principles approach to the problem and confirmed that the system of replenishment sustaining the BEF in 1916 was indeed inadequate. Geddes examined actual requirements in France and then systematically studied the capacity of existing means to get it there. A typical division in the Great War required 150 tons of supply each day.[18] Geddes was quick to confirm that *matériel* moving into France was at a level far below this actual requirement. In essence, the BEF was sipping through a straw when in fact it required a fire hose worth of *matériel*, some 290,000 tons per week by Geddes's detailed 1916 estimate.[19] Geddes made a number of grounded suggestions to Field Marshal Haig. Key among them was adjusting the capacity of the replenishment system so that *matériel* would never again constrain British operations. Haig implemented most of Geddes's recommendations. His ability to ignore conventional bias in his army and invest considerable effort in his logistic architecture had a telling impact on the Canadian Corps inside his BEF.

Lieutenant-General Julian Byng, who assumed command of the Canadian Corps a month before the Somme on 28 May 1916, was instrumental in advancing the Corps' logistics proficiency.[20] This increased proficiency was achieved by emphasizing logistics staff training and attention to administrative detail. Byng was a talented officer who quickly won the trust and admiration of the Canadians, and recognized that they "were too good to be led by politicians."[21] Intelligent, balanced, and insightful, he too was able to overcome the 1912 prejudice of Field Service Regulations (Part 2). Byng, a hard-nosed warfighter, was the beneficiary of a unique background and therefore acutely valuable in increasing the standard of Canadian logistics. His exposure to logistics began early in his career when he served on the staff of General Redvers Buller. Buller was the father of the modern Army Service Corps (Transport Corps) and a key proponent in modernizing British Army logistics.[22] Serving with General Buller ensured that the young leader was immersed in operational and strategic-level logistics work at an impressionable point in his career. Today it is extremely rare for Canadian combat arms officers to get similar professional opportunities. This early familiarity with logistics planning was reinforced by Byng's experiences fighting under Buller in the Boer War. Byng became well versed in the criticality of ground supply, as attacks on logistics lifelines were a large part of the tactics in South Africa.[23] He would not have been flat-footed grappling with Taliban IED attacks on his columns rumbling to Pashmul west of Kandahar in 2006. Similar tactics were part of the war in South Africa. The lessons of the Boer War taught him that logistics was worthy of command attention.

Byng fully retrained the staff of the Canadian Corps, greatly improving the formation as Jeffrey Williams observed: "No function that contributed to the Corps' effectiveness — engineers, signals, supplies, medical, and transportation — escaped Byng's eagle eye...."[24] He also polished the existing sustainment apparatus at the lower levels, taking an active interest in the smallest minutiae of the Corps' logistics plumbing. Most important, General Byng invested attention into the entire breadth of his formation in a manner that has long vanished from the cap-badge obsessed Canadian Army. If you want to make the army better and more successful on the battlefield, attention must be put into where it is weakest. General Byng had a remarkably grounded touch and he possessed the charisma and social intelligence to achieve his aims. The Canadian Corps was much more adept at sustaining a modern battle by the time Currie, the brilliantly successful Canadian officer who had demonstrated his skills as a division commander at Vimy Ridge, replaced Byng in 1917. Drilled and polished under the enlightened but iron guidance of a soldier's soldier, the logistics structure of the Canadian Corps stood ready to use the innovations of late 1916 to great advantage in the last year of the war.

LOGISTICS SECRETS OF THE CANADIAN CORPS

The most telling attribute shaping the success of the Canadian Corps was its sheer size. The corps was large, equating in strength to a small British Army. Whereas a British division consisted of approximately 15,000 soldiers, a Canadian division had more than 21,000.[25] General Currie had resisted the move to triangularization, which had been implemented in the rest of the BEF in January 1918.[26] The attrition of Allied personnel throughout 1916 and 1917 had left the British divisions in the field, "hard-pressed for men."[27] The solution was to reduce each brigade by one battalion so that at least on paper, the BEF could field the same number of divisions. Triangularization eroded the resiliency of imperial formations by thinning out human resources and equipment. Currie's views regarding this thinning out process contrasted sharply with the imperial plan:

> The proposal was also put up to the Canadians, with the suggestion that the battalions thus freed might serve as the basis for two new divisions. General Currie, however, preferred to retain the old organization. He took the view that four strong divisions would be more effective than six weak ones.[28]

Additionally, Currie had seized an opportunity that came with the breakup of the Fifth Canadian Division to overman the four blooded divisions of the Canadian Corps. Beefing up the four divisions rather than stretching to field a fifth increased the punch of a formation already infused with structural redundancy.[29]

The next defining attribute of the Canadians was a solid penchant for motor transport. The Canadian Corps logisticians loved their trucks, and the Canadian Corps had more mechanical transport units than other corps in the BEF.

Two additional mechanical transport companies gave it approximately 100 more trucks than a British corps, thereby increasing inherent mobility. The corps maintenance organization was similarly much larger than anything other imperial corps had to work with. A British corps possessed only one medium ordnance mobile workshop, while the Canadian Corps had two.[30]

This meant that in terms of general transport and repair the Canadian Corps had a significant logistic edge. There was a measure of both combat and logistics resiliency built into the corps that enabled it to absorb the mobility challenges of the Hundred Days. Additionally, Canada's small national army within the BEF possessed the best machinery in France to get the job done, benefiting from the fact that nearly all corps level transport was motorized. This equipment edge was not enjoyed by other imperial formations.[31] The motorized companies were responsible to act as the extension of the railway and deliver combat supplies forward to the horse-drawn logistics units of their respective divisions. They knew in 1918 that motorized flexibility was critical to sustain a more fluid, open style of warfare.[32] In an attempt to increase lift within available resources, corps logistics structures were reorganized on 14 April 1918 with the intent of gaining more trucks through efficiency.[33] Even though the effort to generate more general lift capability fell short, the initiative was significant as it pointed to vibrant CSS experimentation based on thought, experience, and interest.

Finally, there was a great deal of effort on the part of General Currie and the Canadian government to keep the Canadian Corps together as a fighting formation.[34] This desire served to develop cohesion and affiliation among the various staffs and units of the formation. British corps, in contrast, did not retain divisions.[35] They were shuffled in and out of different corps regularly. The ability of the Canadian Corps to retain its subordinate formations not only led to cohesion and ease of planning but also a high degree of affiliation. Affiliation may seem trivial at first glance; however it leads to trust and efficiency when the friction of combat raises the spectre of logistics doubt in the mind of the fighting echelon. Like old hockey linemates who, through familiarity and respect, can take their level of play to a higher level, affiliation or a sense of team enabled the Canadian Corps to generate combat power with finesse. Ian McCulloch juxtaposes the advantages of Canadian affiliation against the more modular British concept as follows:

> The homogeneity of the Canadian divisions "was a great advantage ... they always operated together under a corps commander and staff whom they could trust and whose methods and abilities they knew and understood. In contrast, British divisions moved about from one corps to another, and sometimes suffered from misunderstandings arising from different ... administrative practices in the different corps ..."[36]

With sound affiliation a fighting force can survive with fewer questions or requests for clarification stemming from unfamiliarity with technique. The result is that preparation times are compressed and the physical act of resupply is conducted more effectively between units that know and trust each other implicitly.

CANADA'S HUNDRED DAYS

The Canadian Corps in the "war to end all wars" was a highly prized formation in the BEF. The ferocity of the Canadian Corps in combat and its sterling logistics capability made its soldiers an obvious choice for repeated use as shock troops in the last stanza of the war — the Hundred Days. The Hundred Days comprised the rich operational period of 8 August to 11 November 1918. It was only during this last stanza of the First World War that logistics, like all other aspects of combat power, endured the weight of modern warfare. Offensive success has to be underwritten by logistics mobility. The Canadian Corps' sophisticated mobility was demonstrated both in its movement in contact with the enemy as well as its large-scale administrative movements (away from enemy contact) across war-torn France. The corps was passed between British armies during the Hundred Days like a prized carpenter's tool with the intent of breaking key nodes in the German defences. John English observed: "Time and again, the Canadian Corps was used to crack some of the toughest and most vital points of the German defence, thereby creating the conditions and opportunities that allowed the Allied Armies to drive the German war machine to the point of collapse."[37]

There are many parallels between what our great-grandfathers were able to achieve in the Canadian Corps and what we have set in motion in Kandahar. Canadian equipment, from the LAV III fighting vehicle to the brand new Nyala mine-proof truck is the envy of every other nation in southern Afghanistan. Even with the aging aftermarket-armoured logistics trucks we used, we developed a quick reputation for getting the job done. It was a refreshed reputation reminiscent of the pristine motor transport companies of the 1918 Canadian Corps. In everything we did in the National Support Element we sought to augment this legacy of a Canadian "can-do" attitude.

Today it is rare indeed to find leaders in the Canadian Army who understand the sustainment capacity of their commands. How much diesel fuel does their formation carry; how much more can be amassed in a given period? This is not to suggest that the commander must know every last little detail about logistics. He or she must however know the limitations of his or her force and where the edges of possibility lie. If a military commanders lack understanding of logistics capacity, they will never know when they are taking risks, when they are pushing too hard or not hard enough. None of these scenarios are acceptable. It is difficult to dispute that Canada's "pocket" army was part of the cutting edge of combat logistics innovation in 1918. Through the long years of Canadian military logistics experience from the Red River Rebellion and the war in South Africa to the Armistice in 1918, Canada had built a valued logistics capacity into its army — to the point where it became the envy of other Commonwealth armies and a defining characteristic in the Canadian manner of fighting. Logistics was understood by and important to Canadian commanders.

The unavoidable question remains, "What happened?"

4

Wind Without Rain

The battle is fought and decided by the quartermasters long before the shooting begins.

— Field Marshal Erwin Rommel

Logistics is not hard. Although most Canadian Army logisticians hate admitting it, the so-called "dark art" of providing combat service support is not even a distant cousin to rocket science. I remember being told on one of my first technical logistics courses after I left the Navy a piece of timely advice for a young logistics officer bent on survival: "Lieutenant Conrad, if you want to keep your job, remember to always say *yes* quickly and *no* slowly."

Remarkably, this little bit of field savvy worked wonders for me when I was a junior officer. Logistics is not hard in the academic sense of the word, but it is hard in the volume of detail, synchronicity, preparation, and planning that is essential for success. All logistics problems, whether they occur in a corporate enterprise or on the battlefield, boil down to a few timeless truths. They can be overcome either by directing more time or more resources to the challenge. This is the great secret of the successful logistician; ridiculously simple in its nakedness. Unfortunately things so well expressed are difficult to tease into reality. Time and quantity were never our friends in Kandahar. Unlike the Somme, lines of communication could take advantage neither of a large seaport like Boulogne to pile up massive quantities of goods nor a sprawling inland railway to ferry *matériel* forward quickly.[38] Rather, our logistics needs had to be clinically prioritized through a narrow air bridge between KAF and Camp Mirage on the Arabian Peninsula. The capacity of the air bridge was dictated by the payload of the remarkable C-130 Hercules aircraft and its ability to carry desperately needed *matériel* and munitions into Afghanistan.[39] Though the Hercules has marvellous capabilities, a reliance upon aircraft only for resupply is a hard limitation to have when fighting in remote lands. There could be no brute logistics stockpiling on KAF as our Second World War predecessors created in Normandy. One can appreciate how intensely interested we were in quantity; how much of any given *matériel* we had on hand; and how quickly it evaporated during combat operations.

After the First World War, Canada's citizen army returned to its peacetime posture and units disbanded as the country demobilized. A small permanent force (what we call today the regular component of the Canadian Forces) remained standing as a cadre of military professionals. Typical of a cadre-based army, training between the world wars was focused on small-unit exercises. Not much money was available for defence expenditure between the big wars of the twentieth century. Evolutionary change, particularly mechanization, became the driving force behind logistics advances for armies all over the globe. The incremental changes to logistics units in Canada since 1918 can really be divided into two broad camps: technological innovation and the pure requirement to generate forces for operations.

It is easy to overlook the enormous impact the truck has had on modern armies. One of the easiest ways to satisfy an equation where more time and resources are needed was to mechanize logistics units. In so doing, support units could shorten the amount of time it took to do a task and be able to provide more trips. If truth be told, a combat unit can never have too many trucks supporting it. Even with qualitative and quantitative advantages, the Canadian divisional logistics staffs in the First World War found that their magnificent corps was still short of transport. Canadian Corps staff planners had glimpsed in 1917 the unquenchable thirst of the industrialized battlefield for motorized lift. A horse is capable of only so much work in a given day and susceptible to bowed tendons, broken limbs, loss of life ... and weight loss. As farmers well know, a horse will consume as much as 20 percent of its body weight in fodder every day. It is easy to understand why a horse operating in the Canadian division supply columns of the First World War would struggle to keep its weight up. I remember being mightily impressed in 1994 when I toured the Little Big Horn battlefield with my family. A scrawny General Custer recreator gave us a briefing on fodder and how it was key to mission success on the frontier of the Old West, because adequate supplies kept the horses fit enough to get the job done. Imagine, if you will, having to carry the moral pressures of leading your troops and defeating the enemy, while worrying about something as earthy and minute as your horse evaporating underneath you? Tough, wiry cavalry men like the diminutive Custer were ideal because the lighter the warrior the less wear and tear on the war horse. The underappreciated truck could withstand all these organic ails. D.J. Goodspeed succinctly voiced the need for mechanization to realize the full potential of combat logistics first grasped in the fledgling motor transport units of the First World War:

> This problem of maintaining the momentum of an attack was never entirely solved in the First World War, for the technological difficulties were too great. The key to its solution, of course, was the internal combustion engine, which made possible the mechanization of transport and support services.[40]

During the Second World War, support units grew into full maturity in the respect that the truck for the most part eclipsed the horse as the primary logistics engine. Mechanization of the army was here to stay. The permanent logistics units of the Canadian Army post–First World War were not able to work on large formation (brigade and division level) training but they were able to address the technology gap. It has been said that the U.S. Civil War was the first railway war; the first major conflict where armies could be moved in huge volume over long distances with the assistance of the great iron beast. The most obvious limitation to rail of course is that it lies where it lies. Moving men and *matériel* is dictated by where the rail lines run. The truck had served notice of an even greater possibility in the First World War. It had demonstrated an ability to unshackle large armies from the inflexibility of fixed rail lines,[41] a very good thing for us in Kandahar. In all of Afghanistan there are only 24 kilometres of rail and they are not in southern Afghanistan where the Canadians are. Without dedicated Canadian aviation, we too were forced to rely on the truck as our grandfathers had in the Second World War. As discussed in the previous chapter, the Canadian Corps in the First World War had far more mechanical truck units than other British corps. Unfortunately at the end of the war, only our soldiers came home. Most of the major equipment was left in France, and the small amount of major equipment that did make its way back to Canada was either worn out or obsolete by the early 1930s.

Lieutenant-Colonel Pat Hennessey, a Royal Canadian Army Service Corps officer (the transport corps of the army), had served extensively in and around the thunder of the First World War. He was the dominant army thinker who grasped that supporting units had to have the same level of mobility as the fighting units as well as the greatest possible speed to underwrite offensive flexibility. Hennessey proved to be a driving force for the mechanization of Canadian logistics units. Pat Hennessey is a shadowy figure in Canadian military history, a logistics leader who led from the front and held the confidence of his peers across the various combat arms of the army. Hennessey, from what remnants remain of him in our history, seemed to have been that rare blend of leadership, bravery, and intellectual acumen. He played a prominent role in the reorganization and modernization of the replenishment system between the wars.[42] There is no doubt that he would have served Canadian logistics greatly after the Second World War if he had not been killed early in the war during the fall of Hong Kong. There have not been many Canadian logistics leaders like him since his death in 1941. Canada's meagre defence budget could neither afford nor justify the purchase of mechanical logistics vehicles, however, this did not deter Hennessey. Like a watchful home owner keeping an eye on a neighbour's expensive home renovation, he watched support developments in the United Kingdom. In this fashion Hennessey was able to harvest ideas that would enable Canadian logistics units to transition to machinery with less friction. He ensured that the technological strides being made in the British Army

Service Corps were embedded in the Canadian counterpart (the Canadian Army Service Corps).[43] It is not always about how little money you have, imagination is a powerful aspect in remaining relevant. Creativity and imagination are Lieutenant-Colonel Hennessey's great lessons and they are just as applicable today as they were during the Great Depression.

After years of observation, the Second World War provided the financial impetus to complete the mechanization of combat service support units in Canada's army. The mechanization of the army led to the advent of new logistics corps. Up until 1944, mechanical repairs and recovery were handled inside the Royal Canadian Ordnance Corps, a *matériel* supply organization with roots in the ancient Royal Army Ordnance Corps of the British army. Believe it or not, the Royal Army Ordnance Corps was organized in the twelfth century to produce articles such as battering rams, slings, and catapults.[44] By 1944, the increased mechanical nature of fighting equipment made it necessary to create a dedicated group to specialize in the upkeep of this machinery. The Royal Canadian Electrical and Mechanical Engineers (RCEME) have been with the Canadian Forces ever since performing a miracle a day in places like Juno, Korea, and Kandahar. They are the soldiers who can fix anything from torn canvas and metal through to the repair and battlefield recovery of every vehicle in the Canadian Forces.

Far removed from its complete reliance on imperial support in the Boer War, the Canadian Army in the Second World War once again fielded logistics units up to and including the corps level. It still took approximately 9,000 British support troops to furnish the army-level support for each of the five Canadian divisions fighting overseas. Unlike the birth of maintainers, the practice of replenishment remained more or less the same in terms of design. Aside from mechanization, the Canadian tactical replenishment systems and structures of the Second World War looked a great deal like those of 1918 and they performed magnificently both in the Italian and northwest European theatres. The Second World War in my mind lies at the summit of the brute logistics era — the days of piling the stocks and equipment high for operations. It marked a summit of sorts for Canadian logistics as well, as the conflict marked the last time, Canada would field such large logistics organizations.

The Korean War began on 25 June 1950.[45] The first United Nations (U.N.) collective effort resulted in a determined "police action" to restore South Korean sovereignty. Five years after the Second World War, the Canadian Army was at low ebb having only one brigade under arms.[46] The government's immediate reaction was to announce the recruitment of a special brigade to be used overseas.[47] This contribution to the U.N. forces in Korea was the Canadian Army Special Force, which eventually consisted of the 25th Canadian Infantry Brigade and a commensurate dollop of combat service support elements. These logistic assets were: 54 Transport Company, Royal Canadian Army Service Corps (RCASC); 25 Infantry Brigade Ordnance Company, Royal Canadian Ordnance Corps (RCOC); and 191 Infantry Workshop, RCEME. The logistics units sustained Canadian elements operating independently in Korea until the stand up of the Commonwealth Division in July 1951. Once the Commonwealth Division became a reality, 54 Transport Company became part of the Commonwealth Divisional Column along with two Royal Army Service Corps companies, 25 Brigade Ordnance Company was welded to its British counterparts to become the 1st Commonwealth Division Ordnance Field Park and 191 Infantry Workshop became integral to the 1st Commonwealth Division Recovery Company. In this capacity, the Canadian units provided splendid support.

Korea fascinates the logistician in me as it hinted at the shape of things to come. The Canadian Army was fresh out of the Second World War, an era of brute logistics where we had lots of Canadian soldiers under arms and tons of Canadian *matériel*. Support in Korea was fashioned out of a potluck "pooling" of the logistics resources of a number of different nations into a coalition or Commonwealth Division. Coalition operations inside a multinational division are dramatically different from operating inside a homogeneous Canadian one. Equipment and weapon compatibilities vary even between close allies, different ration preferences, different repair parts all pose challenges that make the job of sustaining the combat soldiers more difficult. It takes more time, patience, and more people to achieve the same tasks that a formation from the same country could achieve. More acutely, the unusual logistics requirements of different combat forces inside a coalition can be difficult to orchestrate. I can only imagine that the challenges that were tackled in working inside the Commonwealth Division were no different from the many we faced in Kandahar working as a Multinational Brigade inside an American-led division in Bagram. At the end of the day do we really want these headaches that coalition operations cause? Absolutely.

The farther the army marched from Korea, the rustier became its logistics doctrine. After 25 Canadian Infantry Brigade's operations inside the Commonwealth Division in the Korean War, the Canadian Army moved permanently away from the division as a fundamental structure.[48] The Canadian Army polarized around the brigade group concept — an overbuilt brigade that was jam-packed with additional capability. The Canadian brigade groups were a compromise of sorts between a lean brigade that resides inside the framework of a division and a full up division itself. They were called brigade groups because they had some of the essential medical, combat support, and logistics pieces necessary for fighting stapled to them. By the late 1950s, many began to detect fissures in the logistics architecture supporting the brigades. The biggest problem was one of coordination among the various units supporting the brigade group.

The service battalion, a logistics unit born and raised in Canada, was the clever answer to the departure of the Canadian division. The various logistics units that had served Canadian divisions so well in three wars had become a knotted, uncoordinated ball in the brigade rear area. The issue prompted Major-General Geoff Walsh, the General Officer Commanding Western Area, to tinker with his logistics assets. He swept all these uncoordinated support pieces into one large logistics unit. General Walsh proposed the Logistics Battalion trials of the early 1960s in Wainwright, Alberta as the means with which to forge a more effective combat service support structure.[49] The trials, which entailed the pooling of the distinct support arms into a logistics battalion, became Walsh's "pet project."[50] Like General Byng fine-tuning logistics in the Canadian Corps in 1917, Canadian logistics was once more to profit from undivided command attention. The Logistics Battalion was formed twice during the Western Area concentrations in 1960 and 1961. The success of the Walsh trials was startling. The new battalion almost immediately proved to be much greater than the sum of its parts.[51] The perfect tool for the job at hand.

Not only did the logistics battalions give the brigade a focal point for all its sustainment needs, but it also simplified the coordination of the rear area security and damage control, a perpetual burr under the saddle of Cold War Canadian brigadiers. Before the Logistics Battalion, the brigade headquarters had to deal with each supporting unit in turn. Clumsy and time consuming. In the new model, direction to one large unit would effectively control the entire family of logistics services and give coherent steerage to the challenging rear area.

The logistic battalion trials led directly to the defence minister's announcement of a more concrete experiment, the standing Experimental Service Battalion in Gagetown, New Brunswick: "During 1963, the army will test a new supply concept ... It is designed to provide more efficient support and greater flexibility to fighting units in the widely dispersed and mobile battlefield envisioned in nuclear war."[52] The experimental battalion confirmed the positive observations made in Wainwright. The unit's functionality was brilliantly summed up by the Gagetown newspaper in 1963: "You'd walk up and down a lot of main streets in this country to find all of the services and commodities provided by the new [Service] Battalion."[53] Eventually, "experimental" was dropped from the name and the unit became 3 Service Battalion. In 1968 four additional regular force service battalions were added to the Canadian Army order of battle on a basis of one for each of the brigade groups. The structural regrouping of logistics companies into a service battalion represented a significant advance. Here was a crystalline example of foresight, thought, and experimentation. It was the first time since the First World War that reorganization on this scale was introduced in Canadian Army logistics. Regrettably, it was the also the last time that any meaningful command attention was paid to Canadian logistics. The logistics battalion trials and the establishment of the new service battalions were the last true examples of logistics transformation in the Canadian Army.

Despite the innovative installation of the new service battalions, it took a decade of major divisional exercises known as the "Rendez-Vous" series for the army to realize that the division, as a fundamental formation was gone. Having perceived a training gap, the army planned a divisional exercise for the summer of 1981 in Gagetown, New Brunswick. This exercise was called Rendez-Vous 81 and it brought together the three Canadian-based brigades to form the Force Mobile Command Division in the largest Canadian exercise since the Second World War.[54] Today the Post Exercise Report of Rendez-Vous (RV) 81 lies dust-coated in the Directorate of History and Heritage. It has some haunting words for logistics leaders. Essentially, the review of the exercise found that the current army combat service support system such as it existed in 1981 was "extremely suspect."[55]

The logistics concept for this historic RV 81 exercise hammered out a makeshift combat service support system however only bits and pieces of divisional logistic doctrine were used. Over the course of three successive RV exercises in 1985, 1987, and 1989, the old support doctrine was eventually recreated with somewhat better results.[56] On Rendez-Vous 89 a crude construct for divisional support was finally achieved. Only at this high-water mark of divisional logistics application were the warts of an old doctrine becoming noticeable to us. Divisional doctrine had become like a favourite tailored suit a person cherishes after an extreme diet. The jacket hangs in your closet familiar, cherished, and comfortable but it is no longer close to fitting. We finally saw that divisional doctrine did not fit Canada's logistic needs. Time and resources had moved well beyond being able to replicate a complete division logistic architecture. By Rendez Vous 92, the last of the RVs in 1992, the Divisional Support Group structure was abandoned. I was a wide-eyed transport platoon commander on RV 92 serving inside 1 Service Battalion and I had no notion at the time that this big exercise turned the page on nearly 70 years of logistics practices. I could not possibly know that for the next dozen years we would drift in a sea of angst, not knowing what shape our corps should take. The net effect of the RV exercises had been to polish the rust off an antiquated doctrine only to realize that the practices of 1918 and 1944 were no longer relevant to the Canadian field force. How then should we live? Three weeks of sustaining combat in Helmand Province in Afghanistan have convinced me that smaller, combat capable logistics units should be our goal. We do not need to worry about enormous division sized logistics units. Small and mean is in.

The departure of the division should have sparked an intellectual emergency for Canadian logisticians. Almost every word written about logistics practices in Canada since 1918 has been written with the divisional structure in mind. In terms of the volumes of Canadian logistic doctrine, leaving the division behind meant there was no effective higher order logistics doctrine. The resulting vacuum in logistics thought was never fully grasped nor effectively addressed. It seems that many conditions have facilitated the stagnation of military logistics thinking in Canada. First the Canadian Army is small and when you are small to start off with, some combat functions are always going to dine last on tight resources. Combine this with the fact that it has been a long time since logistics has mattered to the extent that it does in combat. Fighting in far away places where you need medical evacuation and you can actually run out of diesel has a way of increasing interest in neglected corners. Perhaps this is why there has been a tangible disdain for matters logistic in the Canadian Army since the end of the last shooting war in Korea. The army has not been greatly interested in improving logistics support to the combat arms because it has not really been in the line of work where logistics was a life and death necessity. The focus of army leadership was on protecting the combat arms in a long series of budget cuts. This tribal, cap-badge approach created a fascination with structure and inherent cost savings where logistics development and innovation were concerned.

Senior army leaders during the Cold War emphasized the protection of combat arms units over all other functions. In fact, tribal interests were so acute that they were rampant inside the combat arms themselves. Douglas Bland observed, "the army resisted attempts to change infantry units into anti-tank units in the mid-1960s because that might have advanced artillery interests over their own."[57] Bland illustrates the pecking order succinctly:

> On another level, all the European based formations ... were fatally weak in logistic support. Yet throughout the history of commitment in Europe general officers resisted successfully most attempts to add logistics units to their organizations because that would have detracted from combat establishments.[58]

In addition to this protectionist approach was a poor opinion of logistics among the combat arms senior leadership. The low regard commanders held for logistics is nowhere more prominently displayed than General Dextraze's cavalier handling of the logistics part of the Canadian commitment to Norway:

> The same reaction occurred in the CAST commitment [Canadian Air/Sea Transportable Force] designed for deployment to Norway. In 1976 the CDS, Dextraze, arbitrarily reduced the logistic component of the force from 1,500 to 150 simply by removing a zero from the established logistic unit number.[59]

This bombastic dismissal of logistics troops by an officer as highly accomplished and admired as General Dextraze demonstrates exactly where the logistics corps stood among senior leaders of the Canadian Forces, a stark contrast to Field Marshal Douglas Haig's courageous rebooting of his replenishment system in 1916. As evidenced in the years of preparation for the Hundred Days, logistics requires command interest and support to develop effectively. The tribal culture that flourished in the Canadian Army afforded logistics little attention. No professional soldier would ever dispute the primacy that the combat arms must command in an army. The logistics arm's sole raison d'être is to serve the needs of the combat forces. However, can you fight without bullets, without water? As trite as it sounds, logistics are ignored at the commander's peril. And here at home they have been. Logistics has been dealt with rhetorically by the Canadian Army for over 40 years.

The series of budget and resource reductions that began during the Trudeau era and ended with the large Force Reduction Plans of the Chrétien administration in the mid-1990s forced the Canadian Forces to find ways to tighten its belt.[60] The Canadian Forces, which constitute such a large part of the government's discretional spending (money that Cabinet can actually play with and adjust), were on the run. Given the institutional bias that existed, the cuts were destined to come to the logistics tail before the combat arms. Always. In this culture, logisticians were compelled to dwell on structural economy to preserve core capabilities in the field army. Against the tide of force reduction and Federal budget constraint, structural fascination became the pale surrogate for credible logistics thinking. Even today, nearly two years into the Kandahar mission there are still officers in Canada who mistake playing with structures and units for innovative thinking. Structural tinkering is what you do after you figure out what must be done and how you are going to do it.

Undoubtedly the biggest factor in the erosion of logistics strength in the Canadian Forces was ourselves — the leadership of the logistics community. Specifically, the Canadian Forces Logistics Branch seemed to be either uninterested or unable to fight for their corps and provide the generals with a sound direction or vision for the future of the Canadian logistics soldier. Instead, the logistics people tinkered with structural, cosmetic changes and flirted with the notion of handing responsibility for the military supply chain over to civilian companies. Their approach to military logistics was more business than tactics oriented. While you need aspects of good business in military logistics, there are still parts of the job that are dangerous and dirty and inefficient from a business perspective. These latter aspects are given little value by the senior logistics leaders of today's Canadian Forces. The logistics branch failed their soldiers the moment they stopped caring about the last 300 metres of the supply chain — the part of the chain that echoes with thunder.

An aversion to professional reflection so prevalent among Canadian logisticians has not helped matters either. The logistics doctrine and best practices that we took into Kandahar adhered to a bundle of pithy concepts — ideologies that have gone unchecked by two generations of Canadian officers. A good portion of its language retains the flavour of mythology and dogma and when you pause to think about it, you find that it falls apart. The best example of these dated practices is the one that caused me the most grief in Kandahar — the basic concept of a day of supply. As Aristotle duly noted in his writings, a thing can't be in two places at once, so we position *matériel* in different areas on the battlefield so fighting troops will always have what they need close at hand. The pre-positioned holdings are called *maintenance* and *basic loads*, and they are fundamental components of the military resupply system.

Put simply, the *maintenance load* equates to one day of supply for a fighting unit, while a *basic load* equates to three days of supply. The *maintenance load* is loaded on logistic trucks (in Kandahar, armoured 16-ton trucks of the NSE) at all times and equates to the amount of combat supplies the entire force requires for one day of operation. In direct application to our specific mission, this would mean that NSE trucks in intimate support of 1 PPCLI would carry the *matériel* needs of the battle group for one 24-hour period. A layman can see the problem already. No two days are alike in this life, let alone in a war, and this truism is magnified in an irregular, non-linear battlefield like Kandahar. So just exactly how many angels dance on the head of a pin? Furthermore the notion of a *basic load*, the doctrinal three days of combat supplies carried by the unit, has proven similarly impossible to quantify. All of my professional life I believed in the *maintenance load*. The firm figures for *maintenance* and *basic loads* out of the Second World War were derived after the fact, after the needs of various days had been met. The *maintenance load*, like a speeding car, is really only something you can grasp and measure after it has come to a complete stop. This concept is not useful.

For most of the twentieth century, doctrine has been a secondary duty for army staff officers who would do their best to forward doctrinal ideas at infrequent combat service support (CSS) doctrinal working groups. The process was far from robust as the doctrine work competed with the demands of everyday pressures. For example, the 1996 meeting of logistics doctrinal leaders was replete with an air of defeat and doctrinal helplessness:

> The Americans expend considerable resources to review their doctrine and re-develop their principles and concepts approximately every four years. Canada cannot afford to do this. As a result, our (CSS) doctrine is outdated.[61]

Did the Doctrine Board actually believe that it could not afford to think? Obviously, reflection on lessons learned and empirical data was not a way of life among the Canadian logistics community. In point of fact, the CSS working group did take minutes, as the notation above indicates, but it would appear that they have either been misplaced or merely not retained.[62] This lack of familiarity with the whereabouts of doctrinal proceedings is emblematic of how poor institutional learning has been in the logistics world, and how little value has been placed on honing a body of best practices. Creating new methods and techniques for operations is hard work, work that can only be undertaken by an author with full understanding of the military challenges. This flawed culture among the logistics community has contributed to the erosion of logistics credibility and effectiveness as a corps inside the army family. While we complain about how little money and resources we have to engender thoughts and concepts, the foot soldiers of the corps stand up and get it done despite the hand-wringing.

By the end of the 1990s, the Canadian Army had dramatically reorganized its logistic support structures, but the move was not driven by any observation or intellectual tinkering. There was no Lieutenant-Colonel Hennessey studying the advances of mechanization and experimenting with it in Canadian units. There was no General Walsh driving Logistics Battalion trials with his eye on a bold new way of supporting his brigade on a nuclear battlefield. The 1996 restructure was not about making logistics in the army better; rather, it was about saving uniformed logistics soldiers from oblivion. It was about the very survival of logistics as a military component inside the army. The prevailing *zeitgeist* inside the Canadian Forces in the mid-1990s was "alternate service delivery" (ASD). ASD sought ways to "civilianize" the logistics functions to the maximum extent possible. Military logistics is expensive because it is by necessity inefficient. The logistics soldier cannot work on a mechanical repair all day because he needs time for daily fitness training, time to be practised on his personal weapon, time to go to the field to learn deeply the skills of a soldier. All the time a soldier trains, time for logistics production is lost. From a business perspective, this is pricey and inefficient. From the perspective of a forward operating base in northern Kandahar it is vital. The ASD initiative was the perfect way to kill two birds with one stone. ASD could take uniformed military positions from logistics and give the billet to the combat arms, and simultaneously deliver cost savings in the provision of logistics for the Department of National

Defence. More combat arms troops and cheaper logistics. It is not hard to see why ASD was so seductive to our leadership.

To preserve a core of military logistics in 1996, the army had to take stock unit by unit to determine the minimum number of military logisticians required to support the army's operational commitments. These commitments were taken directly from the government's 1992 white paper on national defence. Once this determination of the minimum number was reached, the axe fell, leaving exactly 4,343 support soldiers to sustain the army. Besides preserving the 4,343, the restructure broke General Walsh's superb invention, the Brigade Group Service Battalion into two smaller units, one that was to focus on fast moving combat supplies called the Close Support Service Battalion inside the brigade group, and the other (the General Support Battalion) to focus on more static and centralized garrison logistic tasks. The new structures were undertaken as a means to preserve at least some military logistics soldiers from the desire of the Canadian Forces leadership to contract out all things logistic. The structural changes were announced and three years later supporting doctrine was written to explain what the units were and how they were to operate in war. Doctrine, a body of theoretical knowledge and best practices is supposed to drive structural revision. In this case, we did it the other way around. Unfortunately, the 1996 restructure did nothing to address logistics' growing doctrinal need. It had little positive effect on dealing with the doctrinal problems of the RV series and no effect on future problems of a changing battlefield.

In the aftermath of the Second World War, senior combat arms interest in Canadian logistics became at its best rhetorical. Since the end of the Korean War and the departure of fighting divisions from the Canadian Army order of battle, logistics as a discipline has been in a steady decline. After 1968, the senior logistics leadership in the Canadian Forces gradually lost its ability and interest to control the unwieldy Logistics Branch, the amalgam of a number of proud army logistics corps, and the logistics structures of the Royal Canadian Navy and the Royal Canadian Air Force. The result through the 1970s and early 1980s was a loss of credibility with the combat arms leadership of the Canadian Forces. Somewhere through the maelstrom of the 1990s where the emphasis was on force reduction, contracting logistics services, and efficiency restructures, the bureaucratically organized Logistics Branch lost its ability to fight for itself. The Canadian Army since its accomplishments in Korea has not placed any serious emphasis on developing battlefield logistics. The great balance of army leaders have let the timeless art slip through their fingers. Infantry company commanders and battle group leaders have not been taught to know when they are taking risks against the capacity of the Canadian Forces supply chain. And they should take informed risks. Logistics soldiers have not been held up to the right standards of weaponeering, fire, and tactical training. Combat logistics is not sexy and it is not overly complicated, but it will reach out and cut your throat if it is taken for granted in times of war.

The Canadian Forces is still grappling with the strategic damage that ASD has done to the institutional resiliency and health of its logistics. What we forgot during the heady days of ASD was that these expensive logistic soldiers are worth their weight in gold. Today there is little depth in the military to generate combat logistics units like my NSE of 2006. And were it not for the 1996 logistics restructure initiative by the army, the situation could have been even worse. After all the experience garnered from efforts made to support forces sent to confront Louis Riel; after being served last by imperial logistics units in the Boer War; and finally after designing a tactical structure that was the envy of our allies in two world wars, the Canadian Forces actually tried to give it all up. Is it truly too expensive to support ourselves? Can you be serious about being combat capable when you lack dedicated military logistics? So here we are, at the pointy end of a long spear that has been the storied history of logistic services in the army I love. It is a history that began to lose its lustre after the Korean War and became downright painful after unification of the army, navy, and air force in 1968.

5

Why Have We Come?

On Remembrance Day in 2007 at Fallingbrook High School in Whitby, Ontario, an intrepid student asked me, "What would the Canadian Forces do if the CN Tower in Toronto was attacked?"

She had the courage to ask the first question, so I softened my answer. "Nothing effective. It would really be too late for the military to do much other than help out and mitigate the suffering of our citizens once the CN Tower was attacked. We're actually working on preventing the attack you're talking about right now by being in Afghanistan."

Her eyes widened a bit. "Really?"

"Really. By taking away training space in a brittle state like Afghanistan, we're making it harder for terrorists to strike Canada. By making Afghanistan a strong, functioning country, it makes it hard for terrorists and other non-state actors to come back once we come home."

Kandahar. The name drifts across the tongue like the shifting red sands of the Rigestan Desert that cuts underneath the city on its endless western journey to the Iranian border. Among the oldest settlements on the planet, the City of Kandahar boasts one of the last remaining Greek names in Afghanistan carrying the moniker of its founder, Alexander the Great.[63] Kandahar is a holy place for Afghans for numerous reasons. Initially the capital of Afghanistan under the country's first monarch, it is considered the birthplace of the royal family. It is the area from which Afghanistan's current head of state, President Hamid Karzai, hails. His mother was a frequent visitor to the Canadian Role 3 hospital during our tour. It is a valued junction where ancient silk routes intersect. Kandahar is equally prized for its utility of location and its remoteness from the corrupting influences of neighbouring states. These neighbours have ranged over centuries from the various incarnations of the Persian, Russian, and British Empires through to modern-day Pakistan and Iran. Kandahar is also the birthplace of the Taliban movement, and it stands today as the spiritual and tactical foothold of the Taliban in Afghanistan. It is to the Taliban what Richmond, Virginia, was to the Confederate cause in the American Civil War, for as goes the south, so goes the hope for any centrally coordinated sovereignty in Afghanistan. Kandahar today is more cherished and important to Afghanistan than ever. Its very name has become synonymous with the country's future.

Kandahar Province became part of Canadian popular culture in 2006 as a nation watched its little army in combat on television and Internet portals for the first time. Unlike the United States in Vietnam, Canada has never had a television war. Canada came to Kandahar at a time when most of its NATO partners were reluctant to do so. It is

Just north of Kandahar City are the mud walls of a terrace-style structure. Entire complexes of terraced villages abound in Kandahar Province. The walls of these buildings are quite thick.

here that we have adopted Afghanistan and planted our flag. It is here that Canadian soldiers are being killed and severely wounded in a noble chapter of Canadian history. Not a day goes by that I do not think about it. I know that I am no different from any other Canadian Forces veteran who sees the word in print media or hears it on television or radio and cringes with guilt. My heart races when another casualty is announced in Kandahar; a period of Gothic gloom and depression presses me down. Why have I come home unscathed when so many have not? When am I going back? We now know that the Taliban, in the late spring, early summer of 2006, launched a major offensive against our forces in southern Afghanistan. Somewhere between 1,500 and 2,000 Taliban fighters were committed to take back Kandahar City by the end of July 2006. There was no way the Canadian Task Forces was going to let that happen. How did we come to put ourselves between this Taliban offensive and the holy city of Kandahar? Why indeed have we gone there?

The dreams of our nation for Afghanistan are not small. In fact, one could assess our current national campaign as sophisticated and replete with risk — almost un-Canadian in its boldness. During my military career, the earliest Canadian involvement in contemporary Afghanistan was the smattering of United Nations observers, eight of them Canadian, with the United Nations Good Offices Mission to Afghanistan and Pakistan (UNGOMAP). This U.N. mission had components in Kabul (Afghanistan) and Islamabad (Pakistan) from 1988 to 1990. The mission of the observer teams was to watch over the Soviet 40th Army as it withdrew from Afghanistan. The Russian Bear had been impaled on the crude spear of the mujahedeen warriors in Afghanistan and it was limping home. People sometimes forget that the Cold War was ended here. UNGOMAP was a blue beret mission that was conducted at the beginning of the halcyon days of Canadian peacekeeping. Canadian involvement in Afghanistan tapered after the rise of the Taliban government from 1994. At that point, Canada severed the diplomatic ties with Afghanistan, and did not re-establish them until after the fall of the Taliban regime in 2002. After the Al Qaeda attacks of 11 September 2001, Canada, as part of the Canadian Forces' Operation Apollo, deployed a battle group based on the 3rd Battalion Princess Patricia's Canadian Light Infantry (3 PPCLI) to the

Kandahar Airfield from February to July 2002 to assist the United States forces by defending the airfield. It was an important task for there could be no operations in southern Afghanistan without a secure base in Kandahar. It is often overlooked that during this deployment, the Canadian battalion was not operating under a NATO or U.N. banner but in co-operation with the U.S.-led Operation Enduring Freedom. The operation saw Coalition forces concentrated in large centres like Bagram and Kandahar with combat operations occurring away from these secure centres in small pockets. Most of the fighting in 2002 was dispersed and aviation was the means to get troops to the fight and back again. Special forces, not conventional troops, carried the bulk of combat, however, the Canadian battle group was able to participate in some meaningful operations around the Kandahar Base, the neighbouring province of Qalat, as well as the large Operation Anaconda. The Canadian experience was punctuated by highs and lows during this first foray into Kandahar and the international war on terror. Snipers from 3 PPCLI where fully employed in the protection of their coalition partners and the longest recorded kill for a sniper was registered by a Canadian during the mission. Tarnak Farms, a training ground just south of KAF, stands out as a memory from the 2002 operation. Tarnak was the site of the tragic friendly fire incident from an American aircraft that caused the deaths of four members of 3 PPCLI. In my time, Tarnak Farms was associated with safety. The area served as a secure place for us to conduct additional convoy practices for our troops before we took to the roads of Kandahar. Tarnak's connotation in Canadian history will probably always be with that dark, earlier incident. After 3 PPCLI came home in the summer of 2002, Canada's army left Afghanistan for nearly a year.

As 3 PPCLI was digging itself into the perimeter of KAF in southern Afghanistan, a second front was slowly opening in the north in the form of NATO's International Security Assistance Force (ISAF). United Nations Security Council Resolution 1386 passed on 20 December 2001 had authorized ISAF to operate in Afghanistan. The United Kingdom was the first nation to lead this new NATO mission from December 2001 to June 2002. ISAF at that point had a firm focus on the capital of Kabul. The official ISAF mandate, separate and distinct from Operation Enduring Freedom, was to help the new transitional government in Afghanistan

An additional view of the terraced dwelling north of Kandahar City.

get on its feet and establish legitimate control of the country. ISAF's first order of business was to assist the newly appointed interim president of Afghanistan with the projection of security and sovereignty in the local area around the city of Kabul. British lead of ISAF passed to the joint steerage of the Netherlands and Germany in July 2002. In early August 2003, the Canadian Forces returned to Afghanistan, now under the NATO banner. Canada had assumed a key leadership role in ISAF.

The current Canadian campaign plan finds its roots firmly planted with the move back to Afghanistan in 2003. In the summer of 2003, ISAF consisted of some 5,000 soldiers from 29 nations; nearly half of this number was Canadian. The mission headquarters was located near the centre of Kabul and its subordinate formation, the Kabul Multinational Brigade (KMNB) was located at Camp Warehouse some 15 kilometres east of the city. The charismatic Canadian General Andrew Leslie served as the deputy commander of ISAF, while Brigadier-General Pete Devlin commanded the Multinational Brigade with a predominantly Canadian headquarters staff based on 2 Canadian Mechanized Brigade Group in Petawawa, Ontario. Pete Devlin, a product of the Royal Canadian

Regiment, is an affable, intensely likeable man with a homespun leadership style. Whenever I spent time around him during the workup training for the first Kabul mission in the winter of 2003 he projected an ironclad competence wrapped in that ever-approachable demeanour. In all respects, Devlin was a good choice to command something as culturally baroque as a Multinational Brigade.

The first line units introduced into the NATO Kabul mission were the 3rd Battalion, Royal Canadian Regiment, a light infantry unit, and its integrated National Support Element formed from the nucleus of 2 Service Battalion. Both of these units were based in Petawawa, Ontario. In Kabul these units were co-located in the shadow of the Afghan king's palace in the southern part of the city at the pristine, Canadian-designed Camp Julien. Camp Julien, probably the most ergonomic and functional of any Canadian operational base in our history, served as the hub in the centre of a wheel for Canadian units. The Canadian area of operation was approximately 400 square kilometres in size, quite small. The size of the area of operations coupled with the military's desire to maximize the numbers of combat arms soldiers led to the unusual but historic decision to pool the logistics soldiers of both the infantry battle group and the NSE into one unit. It was a decision that would have deep and negative impacts. The administration company of 3 RCR, the part of an infantry battalion that takes care of the battalion's immediate logistical needs ranging from equipment repair and recovery through to the provision of supplies was combined with the NSE (the logistics battalion that serves as the logistics bridge between Canada and the infantry battle group) to form one central logistics unit to do it all. In a civilian context, this move was like combining manufacturing, shipping, and sales entities in one enterprise. It was a measure adopted for the specific time and place — the small Canadian area of operations inside the city of Kabul. The support distances for the Kabul-based NSE were limited and this ad hoc logistic construct worked well throughout Operation Athena. It came to be known as the Kabul Model NSE and most unwisely was used by the army as the basic building block for all logistics planning for future missions.

From the summer of 2003 to the late fall of 2005, Canada participated in Kabul as part of NATO's ISAF. All the while, the U.S. forces engaged in Operation Enduring Freedom waged war in southern Afghanistan against the last remnants of the Taliban. NATO, ISAF and the U.S. Operation Enduring Freedom's Combined Forces Command Afghanistan (CFC-A, Operation Enduring Freedom's top headquarters in the country) co-existed in Afghanistan as separate and distinct missions. After the successes of ISAF began to accrue, the NATO mission in the north gradually took on the timbre of the old peacekeeping missions of the late 1980s and 1990s. Kabul made tremendous strides in terms of security. In the south even though the Taliban had been reduced to a guerrilla-style insurgency to keep the region unstable, U.S. Forces in the Kandahar region had begun to notice an increase in combat with the Taliban beginning in late 2004. The United States forces had their hands full. Clearly, the greater need for soldiers was in the south to eradicate the growing insurgency. At the political level foreign ministers had grasped that no one likes to have two bosses. The NATO governments agreed that a determined effort was required to integrate Operation Enduring Freedom in the volatile south with the NATO mission in the north to create one mandate, one clear aim in the country instead of two similar but noticeably different ones. The by-product of achieving this singular mandate would be to take some pressure off U.S. forces that were stretched thinly because of that country's enormous commitment in Iraq.

The NATO plan to take a greater load in Afghanistan was to absorb the jurisdiction of Operation Enduring Freedom in a methodical manner. By late 2005, NATO had successfully extended its responsibility from Kabul to the northeastern and northwestern chunks of Afghanistan under ISAF Stage I and Stage II expansion. Now all that remained was the daunting task to expand NATO jurisdiction to the two most volatile remaining pieces of Afghanistan. These areas were called Regional Commands South and East of Combined Forces Command-Afghanistan, Regional Command South being the hottest region of Afghanistan. Regional Command South, which consisted of five Afghan provinces (including Canada's responsibility, Kandahar Province), was to be transferred to NATO as part of ISAF Stage III Expansion on 31 July 2006 with Regional Command East in November 2006 as ISAF Stage IV. With the completion of ISAF Stage IV, NATO responsibilities would cover the entire country and relieve the United States from the significant commitment of Operation Enduring Freedom. Two different missions would become one and a uniform, homogeneous military effort would be achieved in Afghanistan. The challenge for NATO was to find among its members, a country that was willing and politically able to head into the difficult southern region.

The Arghandab River flows from the north through the western edge of Kandahar City and out toward Panjwayi and the Zhari Districts. I always felt our convoys were at increased peril when we moved west of the river. On this western edge every kilometre brings you closer to the Taliban stronghold at Pashmul. This shot was taken from the LAV III of Major Todd Strickland.

The Canadian government decided in 2004 to play a major role in paving the way for NATO in Regional Command South, as part of the leading edge of ISAF Stage III transition. Personally, I was shocked at the Canadian decision; it was so different from the risk-averse trends of past governments in the careful placement of Canadian Forces in the world's trouble spots. The significance of this strategic decision cannot be overstated and is indeed lost on a great number of Canadians here at home. The Canadian government was deliberately sending its military into harm's way. More important, Canada was shouldering an enormous leadership role inside the NATO alliance with this strategic decision. The new role demanded a geographical move from Kabul to Kandahar, some 960 kilometres to the south, and a refocus of the Canadian military effort from stabilization in Kabul to the likelihood of sustained combat in Kandahar Province. For a significant part of 2006, Canada would once again be under the direction of Operation Enduring Freedom, preparing, from the inside, the groundwork for NATO to assume control. It was a bold strategic decision in terms of both the Canadian level of commitment to Afghanistan as well as the redefinition of the Canadian role inside of a NATO alliance that was reluctant to send troops into harm's way. I cannot tell you how many times as a Canadian officer I have been needled at NATO meetings in Brussels or elsewhere by colleagues from other nations. The common joke was that no one other than Luxembourg spent less on defence than Canada. Canada is not the butt of these jokes now. We stand in very tight company in southern Afghanistan.

The Canadian plan was (and still is at time of writing) to use a whole-of-government approach to assist the Islamic Republic of Afghanistan. Known as the "3-D" strategy (defence, diplomacy, and development), the plan is multifaceted with the Canadian Forces, Canadian International Development Agency (CIDA), and the Department of Foreign Affairs and International Trade (DFAIT) as the primary partners for helping Afghanistan rebuild. It is sophisticated in the respect that the government acknowledges the limitation of the military in bringing lasting peace to Afghanistan. Enduring stability in Afghanistan cannot be achieved by the military. We cannot kill our way out of this issue, as there is an endless supply of angry young men to be lured by extremist groups like the Taliban. The Canadian plan, which is similar if not exactly identical to those of our NATO Allies, acknowledges the need for militarily furnished security but force is not intended to be the point of emphasis. Key to Canadian success in Afghanistan is the deep resonating effects of building a strong economy and mechanisms of good governance that are recognizable and comfortable to the people of Afghanistan.

The nuts and bolts of the Canadian military commitment to the ISAF Stage III transition would include the bulk of a Multinational Brigade headquarters to relieve the United States 173 Airborne Brigade and a state-of-the-art LAV III infantry battle group with all the supporting communications, engineer, and logistics services required to keep it in fighting trim. The Canadian battle group was earmarked for Kandahar, one of the hottest of the five provinces that make up volatile Regional Command South. The timeframe to conduct this shift was set for the winter of 2006. In February 2006 Canada deployed a brigade headquarters, a battle group, a national command HQ, and my logistics battalion, the NSE, to Kandahar Airfield. From 1 March to 31 July 2006, the Canadian troops operating in Kandahar served under the mandate of Operation Enduring Freedom in Regional Command South. It was only on 31 July 2006 that the torch passed to NATO and the Canadians in Kandahar once again became part of NATO's ISAF.

A year after I came home from Kandahar I pulled into a drive-thru lane in North York for a quick meal. I was late leaving work at the big Toronto army headquarters and still in my combat uniform. When I pulled forward to pay, the attendant gasped.

"Are you a soldier?" she asked.

"I am indeed."

"Have you served overseas?"

"Yes, Cambodia, Bosnia, and Afghanistan."

"When in Afghanistan?"

"Last year. Seven months. Kandahar."

"I am from Jalalabad."

"It's great to meet you," I said. "Afghanistan is such a beautiful country."

"No, no, too much sand and fighting —" She was interrupted by the next drive-through order ringing in her headset, then said as I moved forward, "Hey, I love you guys."

"We love you, too!" I yelled back to her. I don't think it's too much of an overstatement. Canadian troops in my experience are extremely fond of the Afghans. The Afghans, however, aren't the main reason why Canadian soldiers serve there.

There is no end of solid strategic reasons for a prosperous G8 nation such as Canada to be involved in Afghanistan. If you accept that the world is at war with international terrorism and non-state actors such as Al Qaeda, doesn't it follow that a country like ours would do its part to turn the tide? The Afghans are a deserving, forthright people who have earned the right to a more peaceful existence. There is still a huge undeclared part of the populace that supports President Karzai's government and the NATO mission, but they are afraid to do so openly. Incidents like the 15 June 2006 bus attack keep their reticence alive, but their larger concern is that NATO will leave again soon. We have always left in the past.

At the end of the day each and every Canadian soldier has to confirm in his or her own mind that the cause is just. You may die here and the reasons put forth by the government never match with the reasons of a soldier. As deserving as the Afghans are, there are few soldiers among us who have not gone there for Canada. Defence of our nation from terrorists who formerly used Afghanistan as a training area is the main

Another view of Arghandab River taken from the LAV III of Major Todd Strickland.

reason most of us have come. I happily stapled my life to this cause. While Canadian men and women ply the inadequate roads of southern Afghanistan in LAV IIIs and heavy logistics trucks, you can rest assured that Al Qaeda is not running training events. We fervently hope that the Islamic Republic of Afghanistan finds firm footing and becomes the solid, healthy country that their citizens deserve but at the end of the day the soldiers are here for Canada. That is why we have come.

PART —————

2

6

We Three Hundred

*It may be that this [logistics] requires not any great strategic genius
but only plain hard work and cold calculation. While absolutely basic,
this kind of calculation does not appeal to the imagination, which
may be one reason why it is so often ignored by military historians.*[64]
— Martin van Creveld

The beginnings of all things are small. My earliest inkling that I was
bound for the Kandahar mission was a short personal letter from
Major-General Stu Beare in May 2005. General Beare, a capable and
immensely likeable artillery officer, was the commander of the Land
Forces Western Area in Edmonton at the time. As the commander of
Canada's western land forces Beare had the responsibility of preparing
the first contingent to go into RC South. I was serving as a staff officer
in Land Forces Central Area, the large army headquarters at Downsview
in Toronto. Major-General Beare's letter was manna from heaven. The
document succinctly described what lay in front of me. Upon assum-
ing command in the early summer of 2005 of 1 Service Battalion, the
western army logistics unit in Edmonton, I would prepare and lead the
logistics battalion (NSE) destined for Kandahar in February 2006. I was
overjoyed with the letter. Battalion command and an operational tour! A
lieutenant-colonel in the contemporary Canadian Army cannot wish for
a better set of circumstances.

I first met my soldiers on a completely different airfield than KAF. I
assumed command of 1 Service Battalion on 24 June 2005, adjacent the

old air force runway at the Edmonton Base. It must have been the cold-est June day in Edmonton's history as the wind howled across the parade square taking service berets and civilian hats along with it. I look back on that freezing first day with my blue knuckles on the hilt of my sword and my runny nose and wonder if it was a portent of things to come. Were Shakespeare's three witches gazing into a cauldron just out of sight of the parade square, cackling about the challenges Kandahar would throw at us just as they foretold Macbeth's tragic fate? If there were witches present, it was impossible to hear them over the biting wind.

It was late June and the entire stand of spectators behind the dais was shaking in collective misery. As soon as the last echoes of the change of command ceremony died out and the blood started to return to my extremities, I began to prepare the logistic architecture that would carry our task force to southern Afghanistan. The Brigade Reconnaissance Team was set to leave for Afghanistan in one month's time.

My partner in this venture was Lieutenant-Colonel Ian Hope, a gifted infantry leader. Ian Hope was to command the combatant part of the task force, the 1 PPCLI Battle Group that he would soon christen "Task Force Orion." My NSE, would serve as the integral logistics com-pany of 1 PPCLI as well as the main sustainment platform for all Can-adians in Afghanistan. As things stood in the fall of 2005, Hope was way ahead of me in his knowledge of all things Afghan. He had served on General Rick Hillier's staff in Kabul in 2004 when General Hillier was the ISAF Commander. While serving with General Hillier, Hope had absorbed the culture and multifaceted problems that make up the rich elixir of modern Afghanistan. I vowed after our first reconnaissance into Kandahar to close the gap between Hope and myself where Afghan-istan knowledge was concerned. The troubled, noble country became my new hobby.

When I arrived in Alberta to take command of 1 Service Battalion, Ian had been at the helm of 1 PPCLI for roughly a year so we became brother commanding officers in the 1 Brigade family — Canada's fabled Army of the West. I knew Ian well for our paths had crossed in our little army a number of times in the past. Hope was first commissioned in 1981 as a reserve infantry officer, a sub-alternate in the West Nova Scotia

Regiment. He transferred into the regular force in 1985. I had joined the regular force in 1983 as a student at Royal Roads Military College and took my commission in 1987. Hope has seen service with some of finest regiments in the British Commonwealth: 1st and 2nd Battalions PPCLI, the British Parachute Regiment, and the Canadian Airborne Regiment. For my part, I have served nearly a full decade in 1 Service Battalion. Described by our mutual friend, the *Globe and Mail*'s Christie Blatchford, as dapper, Ian is also intelligent and ferociously self-possessed regardless of his audience. From the outset, it was obvious that we were working on something pretty special. For the first time since the Korean War, our little army would be deliberately heading into harm's way and it would need a combat service support system to sustain itself.

Really need it.

The simple Afghan phrase *za canadai askar yam* ("I am a Canadian soldier"), which we all learned as part of our cultural and language training at Canadian Forces Base Edmonton, became a powerful mantra for the NSE during our workup training for Kandahar. First, we knew that as a smart guerrilla-style force, the insurgents, more specifically the Taliban in Kandahar, tended to move away from strength and attack the weaker points of military forces. With that habit firmly in mind I wanted my soldiers to look and act like front line Canadian infantry on their convoys. Imitation being the highest form of flattery, we sought to make our logistics convoys look combat-ready, to be festooned with machine guns and be indistinguishable from the combat arms in thought, word, and deed.

The second, more subtle message in the simple phrase, "I am a Canadian soldier," was core to our unit values: we are soldiers — not suppliers, drivers, and technicians, but soldiers. The more things change the more they stay the same. Despite technological progress, fighting in the modern battle space still calls for old-fashioned guts and nerve. Modern armies are highly technical and demand large numbers of talented mechanics, suppliers, truck drivers — young men and women who can ply their trade under the most adverse conditions. Yet all this technical capability is of secondary importance if we are not alive, which makes staying alive the great business of the combat logistician. Anyone can be trained to do technical things. Higher-level logistics work like the booking of commercial ships and contracting for electrical services and aircraft can be done by any number of competent, experienced military and civilian agencies. What mattered most to us was the pointy end of the logistics world. Who takes care of the last 200 metres of the supply chain — delivery of *matériel* and repair services at the tip of the spear? We trained ourselves as soldiers first and foremost. We may be focused on matters of resupply, we may be a bit older on average than our fine combat arms brethren, we may even have some beer guts among us, but one thing was clear in our unit: We are Canadian soldiers first, and if you get between us and the Canadian troops we are supporting, who need this *matériel* to survive, we will kill you.

People criticized Sir Sam Hughes, often for his idea to scrub the existing regimental system in 1914. Hughes, then serving as minister of the militia, decided to enrol all Canadian soldiers destined for the battle-fields of France into new, numbered battalions in the Canadian Exped-itionary Force. It seems risky to change the entire system right before you go to war. And yet, very few Canadian units exist in peacetime in the configuration that is needed for war. The great work the Canadian Army does on the planet is consistently the result of creating a task-tailored force for the job at hand. As we prepared to ship out, my job was to shape the NSE that would bind tightly to the 1 PPCLI Battle Group and the overall Canadian mission in Afghanistan. The NSE that would deploy to Kandahar was formed on the nucleus of my own 1 Service Battalion with extra personnel attached from 1 General Support Bat-talion and the Administration Company of 1 PPCLI.

The logistics mission was simple to state: sustain a mechanized Canadian battle group in combat operations as well as a static, non-deployable Canadian-led Multinational Brigade headquarters. Simple to say but tucked into the bland mission statement were many variables and some significant unknowns. Constructing and organizing the logis-tics battalion to sustain Canadian troops in this difficult environment consumed my every waking hour. The clock was ticking and like all things on this Earth there would only be so much time to think about the issue. Essentially, there were three major factors to consider in crafting the size and shape of the NSE: the Army Managed Readiness

Model, the existing NSE in Kabul, and the 1 PPCLI plan for operating in Kandahar (their concept of operations in military language). Step one would be to blow the dust off the basic ingredients of the NSE, which were to be found in a set of planning tools called the army's "Managed Readiness" model.

The Managed Readiness model is like a cake mix recipe. You pick up the cake box and it that tells you how much of each ingredient the army can generally afford to put into your specific cake. It serves as a blueprint for a suggested unit structure for operations. Strong arguments for additions and alterations to the model must be made if you seek changes for your specific mission. I have kept the copy I was given for planning in late 2005. The combat arms components of the model offered up three different variants of an infantry battle group. These infantry units range in size from 641 to 655 soldiers — light, medium, or heavy options. The NSE blueprint in the model that supported these battle group models required exactly 283 logistic soldiers. I would need to keep my eye on any additions and alterations that Ian Hope needed for 1 PPCLI in order to stay in sync.

The second factor in creating our logistics unit was the existing NSE in Kabul, which had a much different job supporting a reduced armoured reconnaissance unit out of Camp Julien during the winter of 2005–06. The existing NSE was commanded by Lieutenant-Colonel Al Bensen, a nononsense mechanical engineering officer who always bent over backward to assist our preparations for Kandahar. Bensen's NSE was patterned on a set structure that came to be known as the "Kabul Model," not because it was particularly clever in design but because it was a thrifty concept that happened to work for a small Canadian area of operations like Kabul. When I hear the term *Kabul Model* bantered about inside the army today, I feel like spitting. The Canadian area of operation was only 400 square kilometres contrasted to the 54,000 square kilometres of Kandahar Province.

The Kabul Model was a unique construct that pooled the logistics company of the infantry unit with the NSE battalion in an effort to economize on logistic troops. The old notion that centralizing scarce resources is good is often trotted out to support the wisdom of this pooling. Instead of the infantry unit having its own organic administration company that received reinforcing support from an NSE, the Kabul Model fused these two entities into one. Taking the logistics unit out of the battle group doesn't eliminate the demand for support. The NSE in this model needed to act as the administration (logistics) company to its battle group. The Kabul Model NSE was, in fact, a passable use of resources for the specific situation in northern Afghanistan. It was never intended to be a template for use elsewhere. And yet that's what it became.

A significant error was committed by the army after 2003 when the tiny Kabul NSE was permitted to stand as a logistics model for all future missions. Thereafter, every logistics commander was in the unsavoury position of having to barter for more resources. It is a situation akin to starting a kilometre behind in a 10-kilometre race. We should never have used such a unique lowest common denominator for planning. There was not a great need to project logistic service in the existing Kabul Model NSE. The model worked in that specific context because both units were barracked at Camp Julien and the infantry, and armoured troops brought their vehicles back to Camp Julien on a routine basis for replenishment and mechanical attention. In fact, the Kabul model NSE made use of some 400 civilian contracted employees to assist in furnishing military support to the Canadian Forces in Kabul. Both of these NSEs, one paper, in the form of the Managed Readiness model, and one flesh, blood, and steel, operating in Kabul in the summer of 2005, would need to be rationalized to derive the new NSE to support the return to combat operations in Kandahar.

The challenge for the Canadian Forces in southern Afghanistan is immense. Like most fans of Rudyard Kipling, I was at least aware that Afghanistan is a country forged by God and man to impale armies. From the punishing alpine topography in the north to the searing white heat of the southern flood plain around Kandahar, from the paucity of well-articulated road networks to the complete lack of railway, it is clear that the country is naturally inclined to deny the projection of large armies. For example, a professional logistician will first look to sea and rail transport to move *matériel* in large quantities. Landlocked Afghanistan offers no bulk relief for delivery from the sea. Everything coming into the country must come to us by air or over the ground. Furthermore, in the entire

An NSE battle group resupply run to a northern artillery gun position. Under the peerless blue Afghan sky it is hard to believe there is a dangerous game of cat-and-mouse played with the insurgents on the roads.

country there are but 24 kilometres of rail. Can you visualize a short segment like this? A sports fan couldn't travel from Oshawa in to the Rogers Centre in Toronto for a Blue Jays game on such a small railway. This fraction of a railway consists of two little 10-kilometre fragments that the invading Soviet 40th Army laid down on their way into the country in 1979. So for the Canadian Army and my NSE, bereft of helicopters in 2006, *matériel* would have to be pushed to the infantry along the ground.

Two-thirds of the landmass of Afghanistan is impassable to vehicles. The region is known as the rooftop of the world with many elevations over 6,000 metres. The breathtaking Hindu Kush mountain range, which rivals our own Rocky Mountains for beauty, extends from the southwest portion of the country to well beyond its eastern borders where it joins up with the Himalayas. The mountainous terrain gives way to great flood plains and it is here, on the edges of the country's central high features that Afghanistan's road network has been eked out. There are 41,000 kilometres of road in the country, only 12,000 of which are paved.[65] These road networks are scant, so they do little to facilitate a Canadian battle group's freedom of movement. The main road, Highway 1, which circles the country, skirting the lip of the Hindu Kush mountains, comprises some 2,800 kilometres of good pavement, very little of which articulates where provisions need to flow to fuel an army. Here is a country and a battlefield that demands helicopters for support and we Canadians did not have them, not the right sort. Our American colleagues relied heavily on movement of *matériel* though the air. While the U.S. Army will mount a logistics convoy almost as an exceptional operation, Canadians would need to run several ground convoys a week as a matter of course.

The harsh climate of southern Afghanistan also thwarts the sustainment of a modern force. The blistering summer heat of Kandahar punished our equipment and caused both mechanical and electrical components to go wonky or wear out faster. The emery-like dust, as fine as baby bottom talcum powder, winkled into everything, shorting out electronics and optical gear, clogging fuel and oil filters, and wearing down moving metal parts at an accelerated rate. Preventive maintenance for oil and air filters must be tripled in this sort of country to keep vehicles moving and weapons operating. Months after coming home from Kandahar soldiers still hack to clear their throats, and the fine dust can still be beaten out of their clothing.

Generations of Afghans have organized the country to deny logistics, to deny invading armies the freedom of movement. This is precisely the way their hardy ancestors wanted it. Road and rail mean logistics and manoeuvrability to conquering armies. Having little articulation meant armies had trouble operating in Afghanistan. It also means that light guerrilla-style forces like the mujahedeen and the Taliban have a more level playing field to contest a corn-fed Western-style army. Furthermore, lack of articulation means that legitimate authorities have trouble keeping track of what is going on inside their own country. The lack of a transportation network of any real import leaves the nation open to all sorts of groups using the difficult terrain for their own training purposes. The same qualities that make Afghanistan difficult to invade make it ripe for the use of terrorist groups. Afghanistan represents the ultimate training area for non-state actors.

My first recollections of RC South in 2005 were its "pie crust" thin lunar mountains and the colour brown. These hills were in most cases ridiculously thin and reminiscent of the features you might expect to see on the surface of the moon. RC South, which included Kandahar Province, comprised an area of 225,000 square kilometres. Task Force Orion, the battle group that included 1st Battalion, Princess Patricia's Canadian Light Infantry and parts of my own NSE, was to deliver security in Kandahar Province an area roughly one third of the Province of Alberta. In such a vast space, Canadian LAV III companies would have responsibility for areas as large as entire battalion zones during peacekeeping operations in the former Yugoslavia. Additionally during Canadian Forces peacekeeping missions in the 1990s the logistics capacity was more robust as infantry battalions used to possess their own support assets in addition to an NSE. These integral logistic organizations or administration companies gave combat arms units their own measure of equipment repair, recovery and general transport, supply, and ration services, as well as the reinforcing support of a second logistics unit or NSE. In the economical Kabul Model, only one NSE existed to provide support for everyone.

The last and most important factor affecting the shape of our NSE was the operating concept of 1 PPCLI in Kandahar. Despite the best of intentions this factor would ironically become the one that received the least consideration in coming up with the final unit construct. The battle group commander's concept of operations would be the trump card in deciding what the NSE would look like. Anywhere that 1 PPCLI would go in southern Afghanistan, the NSE would have to go as well.

Under the Kabul Model for logistics, Ian Hope did not have an organic logistics company. The logistics part of his operation was mine to furnish. In football language we would need to be in perpetual man-to-man coverage. Such a model requires close co-operation and trust between the logistics unit commander and the battle group commander. 1 PPCLI was slated to replace Task Force Gun Devil, the gritty U.S. artillery battalion operating in Kandahar province in March 2006. To give you a sense of how stretched our good friends in the U.S. Army had become by 2005, one only need take a glance at Task Force Gun Devil. Gun Devil was a re-rolled artillery unit that had taken on the role of light infantry in Kandahar. The big artillery pieces, normally the stock and trade of the unit, were warehoused, and the main fighting vehicle of Task Force Gun Devil was the armoured HUMMV. The manner in which Task Force Gun Devil operated was to surge out of KAF for a mission, and come back to rearm, rest, and prepare for follow-on missions. We were well briefed by the affable Lieutenant-Colonel Burt Ges during the strategic reconnaissance and it appeared that most of the fights Gun Devil did were less than seven days in duration. There was one notable exception in northern Kandahar Province that had lasted for three weeks.

I had an earnest talk with Ian at the Green Beans Coffee shop on the KAF boardwalk. Before Tim Hortons and even occasionally afterward, the dark-brewed coffee of the Green Beans franchise was a habitual stop. I loved the dark coffee the Starbucks knock-off served. Behind the rudimentary pine counter were two badges of decoration; two framed prints of Libyan postage stamps from the 1933 Sample Fair. I found comfort in the romantic depiction of an Arabian camel caravan. The evocative North African imagery of the postage stamp was reassuring as it hinted a continuation of commerce and travel in this difficult part of the world. Rommel had been tied to Tripoli on a 400-kilometre string with his brilliant Afrika Corps for want of enough logistics to tip the scales against our grandfathers in Alexandria. We aren't the first logistics convoys to pass through such forbidding terrain; neither, it seemed, are we the last. There was something comforting in knowing that our convoys were part of a historical continuum. When I think back on happier times in Kandahar, those framed prints, physical evidence of the human spirit and the luxurious smell of dark roast coffee, conjure up the best of memories and professional debates. The most important of which was our late October 2005 discussion about Hope's operating concept.

"How does Burt's concept fit with what you see 1 PPCLI doing?" I asked as I savoured the first indulgence of real coffee for the day. Ian Hope felt that the American approach seemed to match his plan for the mission. It was music to my ears. I told him that in that case, I would work on putting together logistics teams that would deploy with his LAV companies to sustain Task Force Orion's fights. We could tailor vehicle and soldier numbers for the expected durations and increase the size of the logistics team if we approached durations like the worst-case three-week fight that Task Force Gun Devil had experienced. Key to this plan was the notion of bringing the LAV companies back to KAF and surging out of there for operations like Gun Devil had. This would afford my maintenance workshop the time it would require to work on the LAV IIIs and keep them running smoothly in Kandahar's harsh environmental conditions. The concept also gave us one of the LAV companies for servicing on the airfield at any one time. A good time to conduct the aggressive preventive maintenance program that Hope's fighting vehicles would need in southern Afghanistan. We parted company and went in different directions to finish off the Tactical reconnaissance. As I went over my notes on the flight home and weighed the major factors that underpinned the shape of my unit over and over again, I kept coming back to the same inalienable truth, the most sinful words a logistics officer can say to his boss: I need more.

To be specific, I need more soldiers.

If this early weighing of three major factors was sparked during the initial strategic reconnaissance from 10 to 22 August 2005, then it was stoked into a raging blaze of effort in the days upon return to Canada. Armed with Ian Hope's plans and my own homework on what would be required from Kabul and what we could really use from Canada, I threw my heart and soul into preparations, wrote the most detailed administrative appreciation I have ever rendered, and applied widely for input from colleagues. I passed my notes to friends and mentors to make sure I had not missed points. All sustainment personnel in the Canadian Forces are generalists, save for one or two areas of specialization, and I wanted to ensure that no vital ancillary services were undersubscribed because of my lack of a more detailed familiarity with their function. For example, *matériel* technicians are the hardy soldiers who can do a broad range of miraculous repairs and construction of items from canvas through to aluminum and steel. Most important, they are the people who can work wonders with welding equipment. *Matériel* technicians are beyond my specialist area and I wanted to ensure that I had enough welders for the inevitable battle-damage repairs.

There was equipment in the existing NSE in Kabul that would not be needed for the dramatically different combat mission in Kandahar. The machinery in this category was earmarked to come home when we would have the time and airlift capacity to move it rearward to Canada. Of greater concern were the many equipment and weapon support systems that were not on hand in Afghanistan and that would be required. My company commanders and I started to go through Bensen's Kabul NSE as if we owned it and were getting ready for a yard sale before a major move. We sorted its equipment holdings into two piles: that which we needed in Kandahar and that which we did not. A third list was created to set down the items we believed we would need in our combat logistics outfit that were not yet in Afghanistan. The laundry list of these requirements had to be determined, enumerated, and put on ships before the year was out if we hoped to have them for the beginning of the mission in February 2006. The ship that was to carry our equipment to an interim staging base in Turkey had to be loaded and underway by the last week of November 2006. General Fraser insisted that the NSE send some senior soldiers to Montreal during the ship loading in late November to inspect the equipment for serviceability and readiness. I thought it was a savvy idea and despite the protests of Ottawa staffs that were responsible for the stuff, we went and had a look. I recall hearing a story from the First World War that saw Canadian horses and harnesses on one ship and the wagons and gun carriages that they required on another. This story may well be apocryphal but the situation it described would not do in Kandahar. The LAV IIIs would need to roll out battle-ready. We could not wait for other shipments.

Additionally, I was short of operational supply accounting capability. The NSE was going to be stocking over 32,000 of what the ordnance specialists call line items for one mechanized battle group. A line item is like a species of animal; it refers to type, not quantity. One line item can represent 100 individual units, and in truth we held millions of parts and widgets to keep Canada in the fight. Hitler broke down in Russia in

1942 with nearly a million line items across three army groups.[66] German equipment had grown into a fleet of both German and captured vehicle types as the Wehrmacht marched triumphantly into different countries. Our 32,000 line items were for one battle group, instead of three army groups, but it was chilling to acknowledge the parallels. Our level of supply complexity was haunting in its similarity to the parts conundrum that doomed Hitler's Operation Barbarossa in 1942. It is not sexy to discuss the supply plumbing of a task force in our little army, but the reality, nonetheless, is that forces fail if they cannot keep their supply house in order. I felt strongly that we lacked sufficient supply specialists for the Kandahar mission. Adding new equipment and spare parts packages direct from industry as we did during the tour only exacerbated the personnel problem.

General Fraser, our boss and the Canadian who was destined to command the Multinational Brigade that held sway in RC South, was an enormously busy officer during our preparations for the mission in the fall of 2005. Direction from Cabinet, the Department of Foreign Affairs and International Trade, the Canadian International Development Agency, and General Hillier all had to be incorporated in Fraser's plans. It was a formidable task. From the outset I recognized that the general's schedule put him under a tremendous amount of pressure. Everyone wanted some of his time. I was determined to manage the logistics house and not take up his valuable time with the manifold problems of supporting a large Canadian task force in Kandahar. It was a good approach as General Fraser was the sort of commander who knew the importance of logistics support but was not overly interested in the details. He knew he needed some measure of logistics, and he trusted me completely to make it happen. General Fraser, in my experience, was a leader who leaned heavily on stalwarts. He would select people that he trusted over top of cap badge or background. Once an officer proved himself; he was golden. It was a trust that I prized. By the time we headed back to Kandahar in October 2005 for our last long preparatory look at the mission, I had a good outline plan that called for some additional support soldiers. The need for more troops was clear and predicated by the requirement for combat projection in a much larger area of operation for the Canadians.

I was shocked early in the tactical reconnaissance in October 2005 when General Fraser came to see me on KAF. He popped into the large tented annex adjacent to the fledgling Canadian headquarters that existed in 2005 and flopped down beside my computer with relaxed collegial air. I started to tell him where my estimate was leading me. The commander stopped me about halfway through my pitch and gave me a firm number for the strength of the NSE — not one logistics soldier over 300! The point was not open for debate. I could sense he had no room to negotiate on the point and I literally started to sweat. The 1 PPCLI Battle Group that would be fielded in Kandahar in February had grown to almost double the size of the Managed Readiness model. Task Force Orion would actually tip the scales in February 2006 at 1,500 soldiers instead of its original planned number of just under 700. The NSE by comparison stayed nearly the same as recommended by the original model, not growing in size at all. My list of personnel dated 21 February 2006, some two weeks into our deployment reflects only 281 names. This was nearly the same strength of the Kabul Model NSE, which had been mostly static on Camp Julien. RC South was some 225,000 square kilometres of axle-snapping terrain by way of comparison. My unit was destined to project the sinews of combat over unheard of distances in one of the nastiest scenarios ever faced by Canadian logistics. Elsewhere on the tactical reconnaissance good decisions were made to ask for an additional LAV III company as well as a state-of-the-art artillery battery, a TUAV flight, and other specialist capabilities and equipment. In all of this, the appetite to add a commensurate dollop of service support troops was absent.

I was reminded by senior Canadian officers on the brigade staff that the support "tail" couldn't be permitted to wag the dog on an operation as important as this one. I understood the challenges faced by superiors — my boss's concern for soldier numbers and the Canadian Forces' pressures for sustaining our forces in Afghanistan in the longer term. However, there were too many unknowns at play here to scrimp on troop numbers, but I knew immediately that I could not get the boss to understand my concerns. With the small size of my unit I had no comfort zone, no fat anywhere on the bone to meet an emergency, much less cater to soldiers being on leave in Canada. As a logistics planner, you take comfort in maintaining a hidden capacity, a reserve that can be called upon to make up shortfalls. Do you remember Mr. Scott of *Star Trek* padding his repair timings to create some redundant capacity for his work? That is us. That is what we do. Carry a bit of fat on the bone for the long winter nights. In our case this might be an extra section of trucks for a convoy or an additional section of soldier mechanics or a reserve *matériel* stockpile tucked away for emergency and peak requirements. In the size of the unit we were mounting, there would be no redundancy, no excess capacity. Thoughts of the challenges involved in supporting Task Force Orion reverberated inside my head like a pounding hammer on a LAV III axle. I failed to communicate how down to the bone the unit was in relation to the threat and the size of our own supported units. I felt myself at that moment running into decades of institutional disinterest in all things logistic: the hallmark of an army away from war too long.

My stress levels hit the roof as we wrapped up pre-deployment training back in Western Canada. I worried constantly about logistics failing in Kandahar. It was clear in my mind that the battle group had grown enormously for Kandahar, significantly out of proportion with my tiny logistics battalion. This was a much more complicated sustainment problem than Lieutenant-Colonel Bradstreet's 2,700 soldiers hitting Fort Frontenac from New York State. At least in Bradstreet's case, he did not have to stay long at all. He sacked Fort Frontenac and left. With the imbalance between supported and supporter in mind, I made two more unsuccessful overtures to the brigade back in Canada, the last of which sought to add just three supply soldiers to the NSE.[67] What I sensed in Afghanistan remained true. The boss simply had no room for any growth to the strength of the task force. We were capped. National staff officers badgered me incessantly from the Ottawa headquarters.[68] These senior logistics staff officers challenged my math in terms of the correct numbers of troops for the tasks at hand in Kandahar. I described my predicament and they promised me support in the form of technical assistance visits (TAVs).[69] I was grateful for national staff assistance. I felt oddly disloyal but I took the Ottawa promises all the way to the bank. Now that national level logistic organizations had strengthened my operational posture, I decided in my framework operation order to stress tactical support. My main effort in Kandahar would be to support the moment-to-moment fight at all times. Regardless of friction and distraction, as long as 1 PPCLI could be served all would be well. I deemed I would always have a bit more time and dedicated national help to solve operational and strategic support problems. It was far from ideal but it was the best way to play the hand after what we had been dealt.

The NSE, my battalion, is probably best described as a Canadian Tire with guns. In the case of the NSE, you drag the store along with you like a package of capability. Any logistic need that a Canadian in Afghanistan needed short of medical and military police services was ours to deliver. Indeed when I made the analogy for Prime Minister Stephen Harper during his visit to the unit on 13 March 2006, he jokingly commented that the Canadian Tire chain stores still carried some guns.

Prime Minister Stephen Harper's visit and stay in Kandahar was a bold stroke that was welcomed by the troops. Here Brigadier-General David Fraser (right) and myself escort the prime minister on a brief tour of the NSE workshop on KAF.

Respectfully, not like ours, Mr. Prime Minister. The battalion consisted of transport, supply, maintenance, and infantry platoons. We also had a camp services organization, a tiny but tireless ammunition section, a financial section, a ferociously capable contracting office, and a welfare organization operated by civilian employees. It was a ferociously capable logistics unit replete with intelligent officers, experienced NCOs, and tough, spirited soldiers. But the unit did have one major weakness: we were too few in number for the task at hand.

I travelled everywhere with my regimental sergeant-major (RSM), Chief Warrant Officer Pat Earles. It is difficult to explain in civilian language what an RSM is and what he or she can mean to the commanding officer. As the top non-commissioned member in the unit and a key member of the command team, an RSM is vested with the role of maintaining good order, discipline, and deportment among the troops. He is at once confessor, confidant, and big brother to the commanding officer (CO). Given the stated role of the RSM and Paddy Earles's unpretentious manner and robust sense of humour, we were destined to become close. He grew up in Mount Pearl, a suburb of St. John's, Newfoundland, and it sure shows. He still speaks with that enviable Newfie accent that has taken on a certain Hollywood gloss with cinematic and television attention being directed into Newfoundland these past few years.

Paddy is not an overly tall man, and he demanded with irrepressible down-home humour that if he were to warrant a mention in a book like this that he be described as "a giant of a man." The fact is he is indeed a giant. Pat had those long years of service experience blended with courage, intelligence, and compassion that made him the perfect RSM for our battalion. His essential goodness and decency constantly reminded me of everything that is best in small-town Canada where our national soul truly resides. He reminded me constantly of the immense worth of what we are fighting for. Pat is also one of the bravest men I have ever met. I could not have asked for a better partner in command. I have said things to him, shared fears, doubts and concerns that I could have never shared with anyone else in the army. He has seen me at my lowest and my worst and through all of this he has been as supportive and bolstering as that Atlantic rock from which he hails. Truly a giant among men.

On 15 May 2006, Regimental Sergeant-Major Paddy Earles (left) and Deputy Commanding Officer Scott McKenzie celebrate the anniversary of the Electrical and Mechanical Engineers, their corps in the Canadian Forces. The EME Corps was born out of the demands of a mechanized army during the last days of the Second World War. A big-hearted Newfoundlander with a grounded sense of humour, Paddy was the best conscience and confessor I could have ever asked for. I no longer think of Scott McKenzie as a subordinate. A talented leader with book smarts and rugby pitch toughness, Scott will continue to have a bright future in the Canadian Forces.

CAMP SERVICES PLATOON

Camp Services Platoon was an organization headed up by my old war-horse, Major Mark Penney. Penney had served with me when I was a company commander in Edmonton and during a seven-month peace-keeping tour in the former Yugoslavia. I divided the NSE along two general lines of activity — a home team and an away team. His organization was to oversee home team issues — anything that needed to be done or organized on KAF. Scott McKenzie, my deputy, would look after the away elements — staying in tune with the activities of 1 PPCLI and operations beyond the wire. Camp Services included the sundry services associated with maintaining Canadian infrastructure on the sprawling NATO base at KAF as well as all clerical responsibilities in terms of the unit orderly room and financial services. This included managing our Afghan work force of approximately 120 civilian employees, my friend Mohammed Arif among them.

I remember standing on the tarmac at Kandahar Airfield during one of our memorial services for a Canadian soldier who had been killed in action. We came to adopt immediately the U.S. term *ramp ceremonies* for these solemn and dignified services. This particular ramp ceremony was held in the early evening. I watched the brass maple leaf on the top of the flagstaff from which our national flag was draped. The burnished brass of the maple leaf was reflecting the red light of a runway lamp and by a curious trick of the night air; it seemed as if blood was running down the brass leaf and into the fabric of our flag. It startled me; an epiphany. This is how our freedom is purchased. Canadian blood shed in the dust of Kandahar. Regardless of the government's reasons for helping Afghanistan, for working on the Afghan machineries of government and economic development, at the tactical level the soldier must decide in his or her own mind if the cause is just, if the effort is worthwhile. We are here first and foremost to protect Canada. Most of us couldn't get on the Hercules and "go north" if we didn't recognize this fact. Of course, we want Afghan girls to go to school, we want infant mortality rates to drop in Kandahar, and we want medical services to improve for all. Absolutely. We want this earnest and deserving people to have the stability they deserve and break the cycle of violence and bloodshed. However, when you get down to brass tacks, the soldier came for Canada.

Camp Services was also charged with the immense responsibility of supporting the repatriation of our fallen soldiers. This latter task was one which they would become sadly too proficient. I toured the United States Mortuary Affairs unit in the fall of 2005 at KAF and received an excellent briefing from the solemn young men of the U.S. Army Quartermaster Corps who ran it. They showed me the U.S. system and how bodies are packed in 100 pounds (40 kilograms) of ice to be preserved for homeward shipment — packed with professional precision and a comrade's respectful handling. This was so very far out of my league. I have seen troops hurt and killed over the years on exercise and on isolated incidents on peacekeeping operations — military service is by definition a dangerous job — but never with this pressing weight of fatal probability. I studied the Americans and noted their casualty numbers including their killed in action. I asked the quartermaster troops tons of mortuary questions and took copies of their briefing package home for Mark Penney to read up on it. I prayed that we would never need to access the superb mortuary affairs unit, but while I prayed, I wanted to make damn sure we were excellent at dealing with the dead. How one deals with death must surely be as important as how one approaches life. It was an eye opener for me learning to be proficient with the technical and ceremonial aspects of dealing with combat deaths. The Canadian Forces had one or two extremely heavy refrigerated coffins in the inventory for the shipment of remains. Even before our first fatalities in March 2006, we had already abandoned the notion of these two leviathan boxes and gone to the U.S.-pattern aluminum coffin with the 100 pounds (40 kilograms) of ice packed around our soldier. Invariably this ice would be mostly melted by the time the remains made it back to Trenton. The details of repatriation were endless: Committees of adjustment needed to preside over the military estate and entitlements of the deceased to ensure families got what the soldier owned or was owed; elastic straps needed to be kept in large quantities to hold the Canadian flag over the coffins during ramp ceremonies; and sending personal effects home and returning the equipment of the dead back to the supply system and the living hands that needed it so badly. Mark was aided on the ceremonial side by Master Warrant Officer Jim Butters. Jim, a tough-as-nails career infantryman who I grew to love, was seconded to the NSE from 1 PPCLI and although he never quite got comfortable serving with a bunch of logisticians, he did superb work with the ceremonial ramp ceremonies and passing our fallen back to Canada.[70] It was important work because more than anything we wanted to ensure we met our full obligations to both our fallen comrades and their loved ones at home. I was determined to not allow the fact that we had been away from sustained combat for over 50 years become an excuse.

7

Transportation Platoon

"One, this is Four. Someone just shot us up. Small arms."

The 16-ton truck, two vehicles in front of us in the convoy, was taking fire. The vehicle was call sign Four on our radio net. A radio handle in a supply convoy is most often just a vehicle number in the column — nothing too jazzy. Four had just passed the news to the convoy commander in vehicle one.

"Four, this is One, roger," Sergeant MacDonald, Calgary Highlander section, asked from his Nyala armoured patrol vehicle. "What's happening back there?"

"Four, dunno, but we've just heard a series of bangs that sound a lot like bullets hitting armour."

"Four, One, this is Niner," I said, using my radio handle as the unit commanding officer. "Four, anyone in your truck hurt?"

"Negative. We're good."

"Niner, roger. You seem to be keeping a full head of steam. Is your truck good to continue?"

"Four, yes, sir. Power's holding pretty good."

"Niner. Okay. Mac, send Orion Zero [the tactical operation centre of 1 PPCLI] and Orion 2 [the Camp Nathan Smith Operations Room] a quick contact report. Note the grid [exact location on the map] and we can fill in the detail at Nathan Smith. Let's keep our speed up until we're on Nathan Smith and we'll check the truck for damage there. Now is not the time to stop and ponder it. All stations 85 [everyone in the convoy] acknowledge."

All the while sharp imagery from the Old Testament continued to whiz past our windows ...

"Roger, sounds good ..."

The radio net conversation above might have taken 45 seconds, probably less. Clipped, terse language to express volumes of information. These are the songs the soldiers sing to themselves as a matter of daily travel routine in Kandahar Province.

As Aristotle, the great tutor to Afghanistan's earlier conqueror, Alexander the Great, once observed: a thing cannot be in two places at once. As long as this natural law prevails, there will always be a requirement for military logistic columns. Throughout the long history of the Canadian Army, military *matériel* has always needed to be moved forward. In the provinces of Kandahar and Helmand in 2006 *matériel* had to be hauled by military trucks of the NSE to 1 PPCLI with armoured vehicle escort. The Transport Platoon was the NSE sub-unit that shouldered the burden of this requirement. The characteristics of the modern battlefield deeply affected this last, dangerous leg of the journey.

The transport organization covered all sundry aspects associated with physical movement from the loading and rigging of aircraft though to providing highly prized postal services to Canadian troops. The main, lethal job of this gritty little platoon of 56 was to drive the big logistics 16-ton trucks and Bison vehicles on our endless convoys. The transport soldiers, or "truckers" as they are affectionately known in the military lexicon, were a stressed organization given the number of convoys that had to be conducted. I fretted constantly over the tempo that the platoon had to endure and the small strength of the sub-unit. To relieve pressure on the truckers everyone in the NSE from bottle washer to clerk was tagged to serve as a co-driver on convoys so they could share the workload with this small platoon. Lieutenant Doug Thorlakson, a self-deprecating, unassuming officer with exceptional leadership ability led this band of drivers with a closeness and flair that I liked. He was the perfect tonic. Thorlakson himself shared a number of convoys with his sergeants to distribute the workload; he was always on the road. I happily signed off on his crew commander qualification when he showed me the prerequisite paperwork from his earlier days in the militia. I think even Doug was surprised at how quickly his memo met an approving signature. His soldiers needed him, not just because of their meagre numbers, but because they needed his grounded approach. There is no leadership substitute for shared experience. By the end of the tour, most soldiers in this platoon had served in the neighbourhood of a 100 convoys — many kilometres where every convoy is treated as a combat patrol. Of the 56 soldiers in Thorlakson's platoon, all, save one, had been involved in some sort of incident involving Taliban activity that ran the gamut from IED strikes and small arms fire through to assisting the medical corps with moving stretchers at a mass casualty site. The one poor trucker of the 56 who had gone through the entire seven months without seeing so much as a scratch suffered silently with the soldier's logic that when he saw his first enemy incident it would be catastrophic. Like all soldiers learn in Kandahar, he knew that the stressors of war can weigh heavier on the mind than the body.

Home sweet home: a 16-ton logistics truck offers its crew some shade and comfort in the austere environment of a gun position north of KAF. Note the bright white air conditioner on the roof of the truck. A vehicle without air conditioning didn't move in Kandahar. So stifling was the heat and the weight of a driver's personal gear that the air conditioner was considered life-saving equipment and not a luxury.

The First LAV II

The Canadian Corps planners in the First World War were fully aware that survivability of combat service support assets was key to realizing offensive success. At Amiens some Mark IV tanks were used during the advance in a supply role as recorded in the War Diary of the 1st Canadian Division: "In order to supply the troops during the attack of August 8th and 9th, it was proposed to allot the Division six 'Mark V' [sic] Supply Tanks capable of carrying 8 tons each and going at a rate of 2 miles per hour."[71] Six supply tanks were assigned to each lead division and meticulous load lists were developed for them. As noted by the skeptical tone of the Divisional quartermaster general (QMG), the true contribution of the supply tanks at Amiens is probably psychological:

> They were of old Mark IV Type, very slow travelling, and of limited carrying capacity. From the purely carrying point of view, it is considered that a well organized and efficient Pack Mule Coy, or a Tump line party could have given them a start and then arrived several hours before them ... If tanks are to be employed again for this purpose, it is strongly recommended that the Mark V be used. They are much speedier ...[72]

Even though the low maximum speed and limited payload of the Mark IV tank eroded its positive contribution, I find its use in a pure logistic role is profound. Logistics planners groping to sustain the first glimmers of offensive success in the modern era were dead accurate with their deductions. Increased mobility, speed, and survivability were essential characteristics for the logistics unit on the modern battlefield. Armoured vehicles have indeed become the norm in the logistics ranks in Afghanistan. No matter what the future holds for the profession of arms, the timeless truth — that combat supplies must move from one place to another over dangerous ground — can never be escaped. The Bison armoured vehicle (LAV II chassis, slightly smaller and older than the LAV III), in a role similar to the Mark IV supply tank of 1918, has become a prime piece of logistics equipment. The Bison has brought us full circle to the First World War in that logistics units need protection. The Bison in most convoy packages serves as both a battlefield taxi and a medical evacuation platform.

A quick word about the magnificent LAV vehicles is probably appropriate here. The LAV III is an armoured infantry fighting vehicle that sports a 350-horsepower Detroit Diesel engine. It can carry seven infantry passengers and three crew. Its main armament is the Bushmaster 25 mm chain gun along with a 7.62 mm coaxial machine gun. The LAV III was the weapon of choice in southern Afghanistan, but travelling inside the machine is no picnic. Riding in a LAV III or a Bison LAV II can actually be hell for the claustrophobe. When I was a small boy on my parents' farm, I fell down a deep crevice in a haymow. After I hit the tapered bottom of the tight hole, I could only see a little sliver of the barn roof far above. The hay pressed me in and muffled my cries for help. I was trapped in this tight crevice for what seemed an eternity until my father found me and fished me out. I remember to this day the organic heat of that narrow prison and the feeling that I might not be able to draw my next breath. In the LAV III, or my own Bison LAV II, I always experienced a ghostly recollection of the haymow.

The LAV carries 10 soldiers — seven of whom ride in the cargo compartment. Once I pile on all my protective gear and load-carrying vest and crowd in with the other soldiers, and the ramp closes, my old ghosts return to haunt me just for a second. I would sell my soul to be the air sentry. The air sentries are the two soldiers who stand on the benches of the LAV and extend their head and shoulders outside the back deck of the LAV to provide observation and security at the rear of the vehicle. They are at risk to IED blasts, but they get to drink in fresh air. A strange bargain, for it is far better to be inside than out when an IED detonates. Serving as an air sentry is easy when you are in your own armoured vehicle but when you are riding in an infantry LAV III as a guest, it is nearly impossible to break into the rotation of a close knit crew. My first trip north in a LAV was on 13 April, and it was with the deputy commanding officer of 1 PPCLI, Major Todd Strickland. Todd is a friendly, outgoing leader with a folksy but effective style of leadership. We had been underway about 45 minutes when I realized that I had to go to the bathroom. Coffee. I had a communication headset on and monitored the vehicle radio net so I knew we were out of Kandahar City. Todd and his driver were debating whether the greenery along the Arghandab River had flourished more since their last trip up north. Todd's driver felt that there was little change since their last voyage. Abandoning all pride and guest etiquette, I broke onto the LAV radio net, "Breaker, breaker, good buddy. Do you guys ever stop for a pee break?" Kindly, Todd had already planned to stop at a harbour a few minutes farther north. Great fighting vehicle, but no bathroom.

Corporal Jeff Carpenter, a soldier driver from a military family, showed me a handful of rounds he had gouged out of his truck's armour plating with his Gerber service knife. "Hey, look at these, sir."

I stopped to admire the spent bullets. Carpenter grinned like a little kid, which he was except for a handful of years.

"Souvenirs, eh, sir!" He pocketed the rounds and went back to greasing the joints on his 16-ton truck.

The next convoy was less than 12 hours away. I prayed the rounds would continue to find a home in our armour plating.

Sending out a convoy on the lava lamp battlefield of Kandahar always entailed risk and we would never send them out lightly. It became prudent to hold convoys until a number of purposes, passengers, and cargo converged to make a specific convoy absolutely crucial. This operating principle was the least we could do for the soldiers. We were spending human capital to get these wagon trains through so we adopted a Bedford Basin approach to shunting our personnel and *matériel* around Kandahar Province.[73] Going 50 metres or 500 kilometres takes the same amount of battle procedure and intellectual investment on the part of the soldiers. There was a burden of battle procedure, military jargon for preparation. No matter how far you were travelling, the basic commitment of weapons, vehicles, and soldiers was similar. Travelling in Afghanistan's countryside by ground was neither safe nor efficient.

Our vehicle convoys ran with escorts — either our own Mercedes gun trucks or LAV IIIs. The entire lexicon of ground movement in Afghanistan is powerfully reminiscent of the Battle of the Atlantic. Like the positioning of ships of the Merchant Marine and the Royal Canadian Navy during ocean convoys, there was a set order to the positioning of armoured vehicles, specialist equipment, and logistics trucks in a convoy. Each vehicle and crew had a specific job in the convoy and during an IED attack. The Nyala RG 31 for example, was a favourite escort command platform that served well from the front of an NSE convoy. It was the best vehicle to detonate a pressure-plate-style IED with its superior blast protection. The Transport Platoon's armoured Bison vehicles almost always served as medical platforms in the event of an attack. They made their trips as close to the centre of a convoy as possible. And our armoured escorts, the LAVs, the Bisons, and Coyotes, like the old Tribal Class destroyers and Flower Class corvettes on the sea, well, their function was always pretty clear: "Thou shalt perish ere I perish."

> 28 February 2006. Our convoy was attacked coming home last night from camp Nathan Smith in Kandahar City. Sophisticated ambush that totally failed (thank God!). None of my troops hurt but near misses all round. Corporal MacKinnon very badly shaken.
>
> — Lieutenant-Colonel John Conrad,
> Kandahar Diary, February 2006

The 18-kilometre drive into Kandahar City is deceptive in its picturesque tranquility. Southern Afghanistan is not a barren wasteland bereft of natural beauty, as you might believe. The country is surprisingly rich in agricultural potential. Corn, dates, and grapes grow readily in southern Afghanistan. The level spread of these crops on both sides of Highway 1 and the beautiful hand-hewn stonewalls please the eye. Dry stone masonry and handmade stonewalls dot the countryside and the talent of the Afghans who render them could be favourably compared to the most solid Ontario farmhouse builders. A thatch of green runs around the dusty brown base of No Drug Mountain, the dominating feature that convoys must pass as they weave their way west from the airfield into Kandahar City. The lush green is distracting to the eye like a grade school student's bold pencil crayon accent on a bland page. Here and there a gathering of goats drifts by under the watchful eye of a farmer. Like goats the world over they are engaged in the perpetual routine of eating and crapping. In many ways a trip into Kandahar is like driving through the Bible. Mud-walled structures with woven thatch roofs, thick adobe walls made of handmade brick and stone, Afghans dressed in timeless looking garb. All appears tranquil, deceivingly tranquil. Nineteen trips out of 20, this scenery will brush past your armoured G-Wagon or LAV III without so much as a whisper. On that twentieth trip, the scene can explode in the fury of an IED attack or a more complex ambush. An hour after the attack you have trouble believing that the event actually happened, so quickly do the ripples of violence recede in a land that has grown as callous to war as Afghanistan. This is the horror of a complex new operating environment for our soldiers: a battlefield that can pass as a postcard. Just as Field Marshal Haig's generation struggled with the set piece "bite and hold" tactics that were absolute requirements for the success of the First World War attacks, so too must the Canadian soldier today be prepared to fight absolutely everywhere and at any time.

The soldiers of the Transport Platoon were in a constant state of motion with perhaps one or two days a week where they were not on convoy. The routine called for a lot of mental toughness. The night before a convoy the last emails and phone calls are put in. The soldiers never talked about what they were doing the next day because the insurgents were highly active in the world of electrons. Loose lips sink ships. Our telephone and email services were not secure. But families have a way of knowing things without words. They know when their wives, husbands, and sweethearts are away from KAF. In my case, the column of silence always alerted my wife that I was on convoy and I expect many other families had worked out the telling meaning in this passive but unfailing signal. After a last communication, individual soldiers drop out of contact with Canada for the next 24 to 36 hours. The night before a convoy a soldier is filled with a nervous energy in anticipation of the next day. They know that as a ground convoy they are the hunted. The first move in our lethal business always belonged to the enemy, the IED cells that seek to destroy us. The morning of a convoy we were always up early and turned in to 1 PPCLI's assembly area. All Canadian convoys, regardless of unit, left from the battle group assembly area — the Bedford Basin of the Canadian Task Force. The ground belonged to 1 PPCLI and when NSE trucks transited anywhere, they had to be in communication with the battle group operations centre. In true "Battle of the Atlantic" style, armoured escort vehicles from 1 PPCLI might be added at the assembly area depending on the direction of travel that day. The latest intelligence from the tactical operations centre would be passed to the convoy commander. Convoys are designed for the most part to clear Kandahar City before daylight invades but vehicle and equipment breakdowns invariably delay us. Rarely do convoys leave on time; rarely do we achieve the cover of darkness.

At the assembly area in the pre-dawn light the nervous energy is gone. You're focused but relaxed. Looking around the assembled soldiers at the convoy orders brief, you look into the eyes of people you love more than anybody else on the planet. These men and women are your family for the next day or so. Your life is in their hands. The omnipresent fear of unwanted attention by now is buried deep behind the whetted tactical purpose of the day. The only thing I can equate it to is the nervous anxiety you have when you're watching your favourite hockey team in game seven of an important playoff series. If your team is losing, your heart rate is generally up and you're in anguish over what the outcome might be. In contrast, when you're actually playing a sport and have some control over the outcome, this nervous energy isn't present. Your muscles are warmed and filled with blood, your heart rate is even, and your mind is fixed on the job at hand. You don't feel the bite of your nerves. In our armoured G-Wagon, Master Corporal Crowder would have some Starbucks coffee tucked up front in a canteen complete with granola bars and napkins. Damn civilized.

"Hey, Master Corporal, do you think this body armour makes me look fat?"

"No, sir," he drones in bored monotone, sick and tired of one of my favourite jokes.

"Good answer. Let's get going."

I went out as a co-driver in a refuelling truck as part of a convoy that was to meet up with some of the battle group troops at a pre-designated area and top them up with stores. There had been a pretty large battle earlier in the day along the route we were taking, but we were in a pretty safe position since the bad guys had been hit hard and were too busy trying to escape to attack any more convoys. The guys we were to meet up with came in three different groups over the course of several hours, so we stayed in a temporary base out in the middle of nowhere with armoured vehicles for security ... This kind of task gives you a better idea what we ask our troops to do. It was actually really cool to watch all the soldiers work ...

— Major Scott McKenzie, "Afghanistan Updates"

THE FIFTH BATTLE OF PASHMUL

The NSE provided intimate support to Task Force Orion operations in Panjwayi during the first week of August. The most striking event involving the unit occurred on 3 August 2006 when Task Force Orion was ordered back to Pashmul to rub out what we now knew to be a Taliban stronghold. Christie Blatchford, the formidable *Globe and Mail* columnist, once asked me after the tour if any dates in particular stood out in my mind. I have half a dozen dates burned in my memory. They play out over and over in my dreams. One of those dates is 3 August, a black day when we lost four fine soldiers from the battle group. It was a week and a half after Corporals Gomez and Warren were killed and two days before Master Corporal Raymond Arndt would die. Sandwiched in between these tragic events was this assault, which shortly afterward was referred to as the fifth battle of Pashmul in Panjwayi. In the early morning of 3 August, two LAV IIIs had struck IEDs and become vehicle casualties. I was in the NSE command post on the morning of 3 August, listening to Ian Hope's progress on the radio net. The situation in Pashmul was extremely intense as the Taliban were using both IEDs and the built-up area of Pashmul to great advantage against the Canadians. Many Taliban had converged in Pashmul during the month of July when Task Force Orion was in Helmand. At the same time, 1 PPCLI had actually started the redeployment to Canada. The first wave of Patricias had gone home and the first of the 1st Battalion Royal Canadian Regiment soldiers had arrived. I recall listening to the reports of Canadian killed-in-action (KIA) and I heard fear and stress in Ian's voice as he ordered both medevac and equipment recovery off of the battlefield. It was as rattled as I have ever heard Ian become — understandably so. Scott McKenzie recalls that early-morning vigil succinctly:

> When I came in to work that morning, I was informed that there had been an IED strike against a LAV and that one soldier had been killed (Corporal Reid). I was still in the operations centre getting the details when a second LAV was hit only about two kilometres away (luckily no one was seriously injured in that one). However, we now had two immobile LAVs on our hands and we needed to get a recovery team together that could go and get the vehicles. This we managed to do and get them launched off KAF and into the battle area to recover the vehicles. As we were tracking the progress of the recovery team, the radio got really busy and it was obvious that the battle group was in a major battle. Things got confused, but when the CO of the battle group came across the radio and said he did not have time to send in a complete casualty evacuation request, but needed enough choppers to lift seven casualties, we knew things had gone badly.

We sent a recovery convoy consisting of Bison armoured vehicles, wreckers, and Arnes trailers (lowbeds) to drag back two of the damaged LAV IIIs from the battle. My Transport Platoon commander, Lieutenant Doug Thorlakson commanded the NSE elements of the recovery column that deployed to Panjwayi under escort of the battle group Coyotes. The column had to lay up beside the Panjwayi District Centre for a considerable amount of time while they waited for 1 PPCLI to drag the dead LAVs back to a safe point where Doug's crew could load them up. It was crowded by the district centre, with a decent-sized market replete with civilians. As luck would have it, Doug was standing watch in his Bison behind the C6 machine gun when a vehicle, driving somewhat erratically appeared. He used hand signals to get it to pull over and for a moment the driver did. I expect this was for the attacker to say a final prayer or screw up his courage because he immediately pulled out into the centre of the road and began accelerating toward the parked recovery convoy. Lieutenant Thorlakson walked his stream of machine gun fire up the road and into the windshield of the car and it detonated immediately. Our soldiers escaped with only minor injuries and Doug escaped with pieces of shrapnel in the neck and forearm. The piece in the neck just missed his carotid artery. Close call. Ian and his RSM — Chief Warrant Officer Randy Northrup — told me later that that they heard this enormous distant boom from across the bridge, in the vicinity of the district centre from their proximity forward on the Pashmul battlefield. They prayed that it was not the LAV III recovery being hit. They needed it desperately to get out of the hornet nest. It was the recovery equipment, but thanks to Doug Thorlakson, the logistic troops and the precious extraction equipment were spared. Unfortunately some 20 Afghans were not so lucky. They had been killed in the blast.

I was so proud of Doug. Taking out a suicide bomber — particularly a vehicle-borne bomber — is next to impossible. He had fulfilled the apotheosis of duty; given the precious gift of life back to his men, some of whom would most certainly have been lost. He also saved nearly all the fighting vehicle recovery equipment we had in Afghanistan. Scott McKenzie and I met them at the Role 3 Hospital once they made it back to KAF. The soldiers were badly shaken and there were many tears of remembrance, tears of relief and tears for what very well could have been additional tragedy on an already black day. I put in for a Mentioned in Despatches for Doug for his quick and skilled actions that day. Over a year later, Thorlakson would have a final piece of shrapnel removed from his arm. The shrapnel, roughly the size of a quarter, had buried itself in a tendon and remained undetected until it began to pain him a year and a half after the explosion.

Master Warrant Officer Earle Eastman recalls sending the recovery crew from his workshop with Thorlakson:

> Corporal Cline and Corporal Bond in August were called out into the Panjwai District to recover a LAV which hit an IED, only to find out when they got there, that another LAV from the same platoon hit yet another IED. They proceeded to facilitate the recovery of both LAVs, only to find out that their wrecker had been damaged on the road move there ... they carried on and completed both recoveries, under small arms fire, using nothing more than their "guts" and ingenuity to get one of the LAVs started enough to pull it to the rear, while the other technician climbed under the first IED LAV and disconnected the drive shafts so he could recover this LAV back with his broken wrecker, thus enabling the battle to carry on.

By all accounts, the NSE recovery team had performed brilliantly on 3 August. What amounted to a terrible day would have gone much worse without the resolve of these fine soldiers.

I learned even later that night over cigars with Ian Hope that he could hear nothing on his end of the radio that morning. In the middle of that difficult fight he had no idea if any of his calls for assistance were being heard or acknowledged by any of us. We sat on the deck behind the battle group headquarters and said little to each other, letting the cigar smoke carve up the darkness. Four outstanding soldiers lost in the day's fighting. I didn't know what to say. I still don't.

8

Days of Supply

The Battle of the Somme, those five months of offensive terror from July to November 1916, saw the bottom drop out of the British logistics system when the crushing demand for *matériel* for the enormous offensive couldn't be met. The pure weight of the 1916 offensive in terms of the demand for fuel and ammunition far outstripped the ability of the BEF logistics apparatus to support it. What has never ceased to fascinate me and get my blood pumping is that the problem Field Marshal Haig faced in 1916 was similar, though on a much larger scale, to the one that confronted our Canadian Task Force nearly 90 years later in Kandahar: the unknown logistic demands of a new kind of warfare. What ancient truths would we relearn as an army returning to combat? Canadian Army data and figures for consumption, repair, and recovery in this sort of counterinsurgency operation didn't exist. I decided to collect as much information about the logistics footprint of 1 PPCLI as I could. I had one of my senior majors gather data on the consumption habits of 1 PPCLI throughout the fall of 2005 as we went through mission preparation training in Wainwright. As hard as we worked to collect data, in the end the daily consumption habits of 1 PPCLI drawn in Canada were less than useless in Afghanistan. They were misleading. The LAV III required more of everything to keep it rolling in the punishing Afghan theatre. When we began operating in country, the gathering of consumption information began anew.

I still have at my fingertips pages and pages of equipment specifications and consumption statistics pertaining to Ian Hope's infantry battalion.

There was a time not so long ago that I cherished these figures more than the purest Canadian bullion. As I flip through them today they are a jumble of facts and figures on fuel requirements, repair patterns, reports on mechanical break downs — a meaningless compendium of wartime data. Yet, there is a powerful message here among the mathematics. The message is academic now but not so long ago it meant the world to me. You can use this sort of information to grope at logistic predictability. There are never any relevant manuals for the big problem of the day and in the case of Canadian logistics practices in a war zone there has not been any useful tactical manuals for a long time. For an even longer time, there has not been any honest institutional interest in combat service support. So many times in Kandahar I would have traded my farm just to know what was going to happen next and how things were going to play out. In the wee hours of every Afghan dawn while I reached for my boots I could at least confess to myself that I really had no idea.

Ammunition shortages became my own personal nightmare at the end of my time in Kandahar. I dreamed about bullets every night for months after I came back to Canada. We had tried to corral the management of ammunition into a predictable box and our efforts came to naught during the spike in combat operations in July. By August, the Canadian ammunition situation in Kandahar was, at the least, serious. The original idea was first to ensure that we never ran out of ammunition, and second to streamline our meagre stockpile in our spanking new holding facility at KAF. The Ammo Supply Point when we commenced operations in February 2006 held many types of ammunition that had little application in the theatre. Our intent was to reduce the holdings of items that we did not need so more room would be available for stuff we used. A simple and logical plan. We wanted to be deliberate about ordering bullets. The era of brute logistics has passed and today the replenishment of Canadian ammunition is expensive and clinically handled. In the same way a motorist might study fuel consumption to work out his gas mileage, we sought to understand our usage of ammunition so we would know when we had hit the trigger to fill up once again. The motorist uses the knowledge of his vehicle mileage so he can comfortably pull in to a service station and top up his fuel tank when it gets down to a quarter of a tank. Our minimum comfort level was when we hit 45 days of ammunition holdings. This 45-day figure was the refuel mark for all ammunition types. Sounds like basic, good practice, but the logic applied to bullets is somewhat revolutionary to contemporary Canadian logisticians. In the peacekeeping era, our habit was to stockpile ammunition and call the whole heap "30 days worth." No one ever had to prove the mathematics because ammunition does not flow the same way in peacekeeping. In fact, if things go well ammunition does not flow at all. The discharge of a single bullet on a peacekeeping mission is an event that can have a strategic impact. Rather, the bigger problem on a classic peacekeeping mission is to keep ammunition from going stale. This was job one when we operated for a decade in the former Yugoslavia. Canadian bullets do not get the chance to spoil in southern Afghanistan and this posed a challenge to the Canadian supply chain. How much ammunition is one day of supply? Just how long is a piece of string? Combat in Kandahar forced us to be more mathematically agile. We had to know what we were using. We would need to replenish but how much? How often?

"Get in here and get your goddamn hat on!" General Fraser barked. Only hours earlier on 19 August, 2006, the RSM and I had been asked to his office to say goodbye. The commander was departing KAF on leave the next day and Paddy and I would be redeployed back in Canada by the time he returned. We had run into the boss at KAF's main dining facility and his spirits were high. By 1900 hours, when we arrived at his office General Fraser was upset. The term "put your hat on," generally refers to an imminent dressing down. The idea being that a soldier stands braced at attention and familiarity of any type is banished while corrective counselling is dolled out. It was obvious that the brotherly goodbye interview for Paddy Earles and I had been scrapped in favour of a more one-way conversation.

My gut tightened. "RSM, why don't you run and get a coffee?" I whispered.

He was already gone. It was fine to get smoked on convoys by the Taliban together where I suppose any last illusions about my character were erased or further galvanized. I didn't even give a goddamn when he saw tears well up in my eyes at the small memorial service we held in the tent lines after Raymond Arndt's death. But in a perverse way I couldn't bear getting dressed down by my own commander in front of him. It mattered; call it army logic. Lieutenant-Colonel Omer Lavoie was sitting beside General Fraser. Both of them were bent forward over a report on the small coffee table between their chairs. Omer, a fantastic officer who I liked very much, was the picture of professionalism, courteous and concerned. Lavoie had been in theatre for nearly a month conducting an intense handover with Ian Hope. He had been discussing the ammunition shortfalls with General Fraser, particularly as they applied to the four big Canadian guns. July ammunition consumption had slaughtered us. We were running dangerously low on a number of types of ammunition with the big NATO Operation Medusa less than two weeks away.

General Fraser looked me square in the eye. "You told me we were never going to run out of ammo!"

"We hit a major snag in July ..." I began slowly grasping for precise words in what I knew would be a tight window for explanation. In fact, the window closed immediately.

"You go away and fix this mess! I want you back here in exactly one hour's time, and when you come back, you'll be telling me how this is all fixed up."

"Okay, sir."

We had kept a religious account of ammunition usage through the first five months of the tour in order to determine what one day's worth of bullets meant. This was a tremendous undertaking but with co-operation between the battle group company quartermaster sergeants; Heather Morrison, my battalion operations officer; and Scott McKenzie, my deputy commanding officer, who was a whiz with numbers and quite literally a rocket scientist, we were able to come up with some solid figures by June.[74] Despite the complexities involved, this important project appeared to have gone exceedingly well and I briefed General Fraser twice on the progress of the study between April and June. We had crunched the data to the point where we could say with some authority how much of each type of munitions was used daily. For example, our statistics told us that on average Task Force Orion used a little over a dozen rounds of rifle

Brigadier-General David Fraser addresses Canadian soldiers at a modest Canada Day celebration at KAF. Our stressful, high-octave discussion on ammunition shortages was still about a month and a half away. None of us standing at Canada Day knew that July was about to eat up Canadian ammunition at an alarming rate. Our efforts to track ammunition usage were shattered by Task Force Orion combat operations in July.

ammunition (5.56 mm) per day. We had similar numbers for all the types of ammunition we held in Kandahar. These numbers gave me a misplaced confidence in our holdings. If we did not need to reorder until we got down to 45-day level, then in some cases we had enough bullets to last for months if not years. What we did not account for was a month like July 2006 when fighting hit a peak; when the NSE supply chain would be stretched well over 300 kilometres into Helmand Province, when Task Force Orion's LAV IIIs would come back to the FOBs with soldiers standing knee deep in empty bullet casings. The battle group reporting of ammunition expenditure fell silent in July as the unit had its hands full with the extended endgame of Operation Mountain Thrust and combat operations across two Afghan provinces. The lack of reporting went unnoticed by the equally stretched NSE.

Together these factors painted a false picture of how much ammunition we held in Afghanistan, especially where the artillery was concerned. When we reached our cut-off date for ordering ammunition in mid-July for the next phase of operations, I had the mistaken view that we had much more of all types of ammunition than we actually had.[75] Our last order for ammunition, from Canada was dangerously small. We ordered too little to effect a full replenishment of our holdings. Major Bob Herold, my chief of ammunition, saw the pending problem and he begged me to order more. I got angry at Bob believing that he had not fully understood the study of ammunition consumption and the relentless pursuit of a day of supply data. To make matters worse the handover between 1 PPCLI and 1 RCR was nearly complete and Lieutenant-Colonel Omer Lavoie now held the reins as the new battle group commander. Omer's manner of fighting called for much more artillery shells than what we had grown accustomed to with 1 PPCLI. The depleted stocks we had on hand were burning up at an unanticipated rate. I thought the data Scott McKenzie and I had compiled was infallible, but I had not fully appreciated what July had done to us. Bob Herold did and he had been right. It could have been catastrophic to the next operation, NATO's first battle.

Recognition of the crisis and the corrective action needed to improve the ammunition holdings began two weeks before the day I stood with my heels together in the brigade commander's office on 19 August. Once we had learned the full truth of July ammunition consumption in early August, we put measures in place; we leaned hard on Canada for emergency replenishment of ammunition. It was going to be close, but I was certain that we would be all right for Operation Medusa. General Fraser was concerned, and I felt as if I had let down the boss in a big, big way. I was so sure, so determined to nail down the ebb and flow of ammunition in Kandahar. Omer Lavoie was right to bring the matter to his brigade commander, although the blunt one-way conversation with General Fraser in front of Omer still stings my memory. The fact that we had made such a determined effort to prevent a shortage tortured me even more. The realities of combat and a relief in place between two excellent but different fighting units had taught me more about ammunition than my previous 20-odd years of experience combined.

A full year after the tense meeting at brigade on 19 August 2006, General Fraser and I talked over beers in Toronto. "It wasn't your fault that we ran low on ammunition. The mistake you made is that you tried to fix the matter without telling me earlier about the problem. You should have come to me right away with the issue and then set to work on it."

If only there were handbooks for this sort of stuff ...

Supply Platoon of the NSE was in a permanent state of crisis management to furnish Canadian commodities. The last thing we wanted the infantry to worry about was looking over their shoulder for something they needed. The truth is that some commodities, particularly ammunition, were often in short supply. In some cases the number of bullets was accounted for in single digits.[76] I never wanted Hope's group to worry about this. My ammunition officer, the wily, pipe smoking Major Bob Herold, and his tiny ammunition section worked the phone lines and email links that are the living tissue of the Canadian ammunition world and pulled off miracle after miracle to solve shortages behind the scenes away from the infantry. At the same time, I hoped that by creating the illusion of endless, excellent equipment, we would have a corrosive effect on the mind of the Taliban. Anyone can be tough for a moment or two. It takes a task force replete with robust logistics to be tough for seven months in as punishing an environment as we found ourselves. There is a feeling that the psychological effect of having "lots" has passed with the decline of brute logistics. I do not think this is true. Even in the reduced logistic footprint of the contemporary battlefield there is a tremendous psychological edge for the Canadian soldier to know that his side has lots of excellent equipment and *matériel*. We worked hard to create the impression for the battle group that there was a lot more where that came from even when it was not actually the case. On one level, our aim was to allow the infantry to take comfort in the knowledge that the "loggies" would fret about replacing the supplies they expended, so they could focus on their many other concerns. On another, we wished to demoralize the enemy by conveying the impression that we have a ton of whatever: You might knock out one of our LAV IIIs but we have 100 more to replace it.

Let's face it, military supply is usually an unimaginative butt-end to many service jokes. I still smart over the ending of the entertaining

Clint Eastwood movie *Heartbreak Ridge* where a goofy, ineffective Marine Corps company commander is told by his commanding general to "go back to the supply branch of the Marine Corps" after he proves himself ineffectual in the invasion of Grenada. Sigh ... and I love Clint Eastwood, but I do not know too many service battalion commanders who would want a company commander like that either. Certainly not in Iraq or Afghanistan.

"Bin rat" is the pet name Canadians have for supply types, as in "Hey, bin rat, you won't give me your boots because then you'd have nothing on your shelves."

Funny stuff — at least until you find yourself in a sustained and real war. Losing the grip on your country's supply chain will get soldiers killed. I am fascinated by supply's mercurial nature, the quantum leaps and bizarre ebbs and flows of martial *matériel*. Like the proverbial lost sock in your dryer at home or your joint cheque account that never comes out balanced, there is something beyond physics and mathematics to the art of supply. Supply Platoon conducted most of its yeoman work on a dusty corner of the airfield. This platoon, commanded by the soft-spoken and perpetually upbeat Captain Bobby Alolega was analogous to a thinking, breathing warehouse. It was crucial to keep track of what we had and did not have. In Kandahar we had a scenario that we had not faced in generations — the hard fact that we could not always get more of a given *matériel*, at least not right away. We were small as a supply organization but we were blessed with some of the best supply soldiers in the Canadian Forces. The men and women of this organization kept track of our thousands and thousands of parts; they purchased items that we could not get out of the Canadian supply chain in time. Logistics is finite and in real combat you can indeed run out.

The psychological challenge to our supply soldiers was unique. Everyone in the unit had to participate in convoys to share the security duties of our infantry, transport, and maintenance platoons. The reality was however that most of the heavy supply work had to occur on KAF. This work was vital to the success of the mission. When you are camp-bound and see soldiers come back hurt or worse, or see equipment and combat uniforms returned for disposal that are hardened with bloodstains, it preys on you. The camp-focused soldiers start to think that the Taliban are four metres tall and that they are everywhere beyond the wire. The fear, guilt, and tension builds in the mind like a psychosis and doing convoys actually helps to alleviate these complex snake balls of feelings. The supply problems we faced at the beginning of the tour were incredible. The Supply Platoon had to unpack and sort out gear that had come down from Kabul. The previous unit had done as good a job as they could loading up but it was obvious that time had run out on them by the state of some of the sea containers. The need for equipment for the Canadian staff at General Fraser's Multinational Brigade headquarters, the Canadian-led Role 3 Military Hospital at KAF, and the battle group was suffocating. The 36 supply technicians worked around the clock against this insatiable need. I had made a mistake on the number of local procurement personnel I had in the organization, the soldiers who can buy stuff outside of the military supply chain and in most cases get *matériel* quicker. I had two working in Kandahar, which I deemed to be adequate, given that we had a purchasing shop on our base on the Arabian Peninsula and a big one in Montreal that would buy stuff outside of the military supply chain and have it shipped to us. I learned only through experience that Montreal might as well have been on the moon. This great city was too far for most of this sort of procurement work. The things we were buying we needed immediately. The time problem was only worsened by the narrow air bridge that sustained us in Kandahar. Just because a product is purchased in Montreal, it still has to eventually make its way onto a Hercules aircraft to get to us. Buy it as close as you can and always, always shop Afghan if you can. This was what I learned. Buying *matériel* and services from the Afghans — even if it took longer or was slightly inferior in quality is a savvy way to help prime an economy that is desperately seeking ways to leave poppies and opium behind. In the end, we sent military purchasing agents south to the Arabian Peninsula to help locate and purchase raw equipment for the Canadians in Afghanistan.

Throughout this period of desperation, I never heard one soldier from Supply Platoon complain. Bobby, the gentlest soul in the NSE, was always smiling and accentuating the positive, and his seasoned sergeant-major, Ollie Cromwell, moved from task to task with the patience of Job, lending his experience and energy to a problem as if all of our lives depended on it. And in some cases they did.

> Hi. We are Canadians. We would like to buy $90,000 worth of metallic shelving for a military medical facility up north — and by the way, don't bother wrapping it because we needed it yesterday.

9

Nothing They Could Not Fix

Master Corporal Whelan is a marathon runner built like a punishing linebacker. He is a soldier's soldier and a vehicle mechanic in the NSE. A Newfoundlander through and through, Whelan is slow-talking, quick-thinking with a penchant for cigarettes, wry one-liners, and running. I watched him finish a marathon race in Edmonton in August 2005. Marathon is not an accurate term, this event, known as the Mountain Man Competition is a gruelling military fitness race that takes the better part of a day to complete. Whelan finished the race with a tremendous time then flopped out on the grass to enjoy a cigarette and a pop while he watched other soldiers lope in across the finish line. He is also blessed with a god-given acumen for fixing anything mechanical including the Canadian LAV III fighting vehicle. He can repair them with his eyes closed and has done almost exactly that while serving at various dust- and rocket-infested forward operating bases in Kandahar Province. During our tour, Whelan often found himself living beyond the relative safety of the wire giving close mechanical support to the infantry, who are utterly dependant on the serviceability of the excellent LAV III fighting machine. I always enjoyed shooting the breeze with Master Corporal Whelan wherever I bumped into him. Who would not? He is insightful and never hurried. He always asks about how other people are holding up or getting on. He only talks about himself when pressed directly.

Typical of Whelan, I heard about one of his finer moments from somebody else, a Canadian journalist in this case. The story was written early in our tour, in the late April timeframe when the Task Force was bent on building a FOB (Martello) for Alpha Company in the northern part of Kandahar Province. The brief but telling story unfurled over cigar smoke and antique Afghan dust behind the steel sea container complex that serves as the Canadian Task Force headquarters at KAF.

"Do you know Master Corporal Whelan?" the reporter asked me.

I chuckled. "I sure do. He kind of sticks out from time to time."

In this instance Whelan was the repair team leader on a Task Force Orion convoy and as often occurs; one of the vehicles in the party broke down. The vehicle casualty could not be repaired where it was, so the soldiers prepared for one of the infamous long halts that are stock and trade with operations in southern Afghanistan. Master Corporal Whelan and Alpha Company, the infantry company he was attached to, had to bed down for the night in an area that is well populated with insurgents. The tactical opinion held that it would be a busy night.

"Whelan nonchalantly moseyed over to his Bison and tucked away his [LAV III] tools in his armoured vehicle," the reporter told me, picking up a more useful one for the job at hand. "We couldn't see what he was waving at first and then it became obvious — his rifle. We were somewhat strained by this point of the day. Whelan nodded in his nonchalant manner to all of us reporters who had been watching the big Newfoundlander." Brandishing his C7A2 service rifle in his big mitt, he remarked, "Well, boys, looks like we're going to be needing these tonight."

Even now I can hear him drawling out the words as unfussed as ever, as if he was ordering an Ice Cap at Tim Hortons. The reporters apparently grinned nervously but they felt better in spite of themselves. I was not there that night in late April 2006 but when the story ends, I smile for completely different reasons.

In early April 2006, almost a full month before Whelan's moment of resolve with the Canadian journalists, a different crew of NSE mechanics was out with Alpha Company on a patrol in northern Kandahar Province. They were with the Patricias to provide intimate mechanical repair and recovery but they found the occasion to put the C6 machine gun on their Bison Mobile Repair Vehicle to good use. This time it was not a breakdown but an attack on a LAV III in their convoy. The Canadian vehicle was struck by an IED and in the aftermath Master Corporal Bennett and Corporal Firth spotted the insurgents who detonated the explosive. They engaged the attackers and kept them at bay with the machine gun. The precious minutes gained from their instinctive reaction gave their infantry brethren a square chance to take care of the casualties and patch up the convoy.

I am glad that I know these men. I am even more glad that they fight on our side. This is no country for old men. So often at the end of punishing convoy days I have felt like a living fossil: bone tired and ineffectual. Soldiers like Whelan, Bennett, and Firth galvanize old men to face the charge all over again. Who could not be proud of them?

It was always said of Doug Flutie, the superb U.S. College, NFL, and CFL quarterback that he never lost any football games; he just ran out of time. The same adage goes well with the soldiers of our Maintenance Platoon or field workshop as it is colloquially known. I know in my heart of hearts that there was nothing the enemy could do to any of our fighting vehicles and armoured trucks that this gang could not fix. A fact that gave me tremendous confidence even as the battle damaged LAV IIIs began to pile up in the workshop. The issue on the battlefield is the age-old enemy of the logistician discussed in chapter 4 — time. Repairs that get too involved and chew up too many precious production hours need to be done in Canada. You cannot afford to have all of your doctors working on one extremely ill patient. Mechanical triage is imperative to keep the wider part of your force in the fight. The Maintenance Platoon, like the Transport Platoon had two roles one static and one expeditionary. The heavier, more complicated machinery repairs and tune-ups were conducted at the workshop on KAF. The lion share of the platoon's work, however, was outside the wire. They dispatched repair teams to travel with the infantry companies to do repairs and extractions right on the spot. They serviced all the equipment, weapons, and fire control systems, and even manufactured items using their small but excellent welding shop. It seemed to me that there was nothing these warrior craftsmen could not fix. The platoon was well led by the cerebral Captain Chris Woods and my crusty but resourceful Equipment Technical Quartermaster Sergeant Major Earle Eastman. Eastman, a master warrant officer, was a wily old fox who had a knack for organization and rattling the right chains inside the technical community at Ottawa to get things done. Chris was a good officer and a compassionate leader who cared deeply about the well-being of his soldiers. He made the unfortunate decision to shave his head to make himself more comfortable around the dusty workshop on the Kandahar Airfield. No sooner had the razor finished its dramatic work leaving behind a gleaming, white head when the news of the prime minister's visit hit the camp. One of my favourite pictures from the tour is of Captain Woods, an intensely private and self conscious individual, briefing Prime Minister Harper with that day-old "Baby Huey" bald head of his. I think even Mr. Harper, normally so composed and unflappable around bright media lights, took note of Chris's new look.

Maintenance activity was conducted at a frenetic pace throughout the tour with a spirit that oscillated between extreme urgency, and flat-out desperation for the entire seven months. We did well to keep the tone

Master Warrant Officer Earle Eastman (left) and RSM Paddy Earles stop for a photo opportunity against the Hindu Kush Mountains in Kabul. The NSE had a small detachment in Kabul to provide support for the Canadians who served in the capital. We tried to get senior NSE visitors up to Kabul at least once a month to show that we still loved them. This photo was taken at the training area of the Afghan National Army outside Kabul. The Canadians working with the Afghan National Army under Major Paul Peyton and Mike Gagnon in the capital were doing some of the most important and relevant work in Afghanistan.

on the side of urgency. Our unit size had been capped at 300, but I was able to increase the size of the workshop by reducing the numbers of cooks we would take to an even dozen. This was possible because U.S. contractors on KAF prepared many of our meals and the only Canadian kitchens in operation during our tour were in Kandahar City at the Provincial Reconstruction Team (PRT) Camp and at the forward operating base in Spin Boldak. The Canadian Task Force eventually logged some 1,750,000 kilometres, fought in over 100 enemy engagements, and sustained battle damage to over 50 vehicles during our time in country. This necessitated nearly 6,400 repairs to equipment and the battlefield recovery of some 126 broken vehicles. Against the anvil of insatiable equipment demand, from LAV III fighting vehicles to the aging but resilient logistics wagons, the Maintenance Platoon managed to keep serviceability rates at a level that would be the envy of any trucking firm operating on smooth Canadian roads. With the establishment of FOBs Martello and Spin Boldak and a patrol base at the Zhari District Centre (ZDC) and Camp Nathan Smith, much of the maintenance resources were decentralized with some resources being shifted around continuously to support the main effort. The two biggest challenges presented by this decentralized tactical posture were the availability of repair parts and the negligible time afforded to preventive and corrective maintenance. You cannot fix your car when it is moving, and the tempo of the mission kept the infantry LAVs constantly on the go.

In the early going of the tour the Taliban sought out the LAV III as a target. It was a bull-in-a-china-shop mentality that I believe was seeking a weakness in the superb machine. The LAV III is a tremendous fighting vehicle but it does break when the bomb is big enough. The efforts of the mechanic warriors were inspiring. They would move heaven and earth to fix a battle-damaged LAV so it could be put back out in operations in the shortest possible time. The message sent to the enemy by this approach was that you did not hurt us. Even though nearly 80 percent of the battle-damaged LAVs can be fixed right at KAF, the Taliban did damage some that could not be fixed in theatre. However, we never discussed this fact. Through the superb efforts of the maintainers, we tried to get the machines working again. The effect of this repair ethos is analogous to a behaviour of a football running back after having sustained a bone-crushing hit. He will trot back to the huddle. He does not lie on the field like he would dearly wish to do, rather he jumps up and jogs back for the next play. The psychological message to the defence is, "Is that all you got? You did not hurt me. My equipment has rendered me indestructible."

Stopping a military convoy for any length of time in southern Afghanistan is a bad idea. The convoys are almost always under someone's watchful eye in this antique land and when you stop you present an opportunity for the enemy. Unfortunately, every time we had to reclaim a broken LAV whether it was a mechanical failure or damaged in battle this is exactly what we had to do. When the LAV III was purchased, a number of variants or models were purchased along with it. The main variants, of course, were the infantry section carrier, a command post configuration, and smaller numbers of specialized types like the combat engineer model or the forward observation officer (FOO) variant. There was one serious exception in the selection of LAV III variants. There was no consideration given to moving the heavy armoured vehicle when it was knocked out of action. The army decided to pass on the requirement for a LAV III recovery variant, a machine with the muscle to pull a damaged LAV III off the battlefield when it has been blown apart and none of its tires can move. A cheque written a decade before by army planners was cashed in during our tour. LAV III recovery was a huge problem for us in Kandahar and we struggled with it for our entire seven month mission. When we started taking hits to the LAV III we worked out a manner of recovery using a pair of 16-ton trucks: one was a wrecker and one was a tractor trailer that towed a large, flatbed-style trailer called the Arnes trailer.

Our armoured wrecker and the civilian-pattern Arnes trailer had to be used in tandem to make a recovery. By civilian pattern, I mean that our flatbed trailers were off the shelf and no different from the ones you would see on the Trans-Canada or 400 series highways here in Ontario. They were designed to do heavy equipment transfers on well-paved roads in Canada. When recovering a LAV, the tractor pulling the flatbed first had to unhitch it and move away. Next, hydraulics on the front of the flatbed lowered the bed. Then, the wrecker dragged the battle-damaged vehicle onto the flatbed. Once this was done, the tractor came back and was hitched up to the flatbed. Finally, the two vehicles moved off again in convoy with the damaged LAV III onboard. Although the recovery manoeuvre showcases Canadian grit and ingenuity it was a dangerous drill to run on a battlefield like Kandahar.

In late July, near the end of our tour, CJTF 76, our American division headquarters in Bagram, wanted some Afghan National Army equipment picked up from FOB Robinson in the Sangin District of Helmand Province and moved back to Kandahar. This FOB was in the British sector. Major Bill Fletcher and his "C" Company had reinforced this FOB in May, doing some exceptional work in support of the United Kingdom. To do this transfer of equipment would require all of our serviceable Arnes trailers. In effect our ability to recover a damaged LAV III in Afghanistan would be put in jeopardy. In my estimation the recovery of this heavy equipment from Robinson would be best handled by the United Kingdom because they were much closer, the Afghan equipment had been working in conjunction with British troops. To strengthen my argument, the United Kingdom had marvellous, military-pattern flatbed trailers that were more suited to the task than the Arnes. They were closer, and had the better tool for the job. The United Kingdom refused the task and CJTF 76 passed the job to the Canadians. I stalled a bit because I knew that the Netherlands Army also had military-pattern recovery trailers. I pushed back for a while hoping to force one of our better-equipped partners to do the job. I went to see Major Mason Stalker, the talented young operations officer of 1 PPCLI to explain why we should not do the task. Mason was frustrated because the filibuster was a distraction. He wanted the administrative issue sorted and quickly but to his credit he agreed to stall the task for a while to see if CJTF 76 would reassign it. They did not. Neither the United Kingdom nor the Netherlands would do the task and the time for discussion was over. In the end a Canadian convoy consisting of infantry escort and inferior civilian-pattern lift equipment moved the heavy engineer vehicles for the Afghan Army. They went into the Khe Sanh that was FOB Robinson and they moved the whole heavy mess. And they did it well. When I think back on the things in Kandahar that instill pride, this little logistics job that Canada did, a huge task that could evaporate so easily from recollection on a tour as busy as ours, figures prominently in my mind.

These three Canadian machines have been damaged by IEDs. The maintainers would move heaven and earth to fix the worst of repairs in Afghanistan, and I honestly believe there was nothing they couldn't mend given time. Vehicles with hull breaches had to go back to Canada. Tactical mechanics had to perform thrifty triage. Despite their incredible talents, we couldn't afford to have them put too much time into any one vehicle. The Mercedes G-Wagon on the right was sent home in a sea container during our tour. It was recently featured in an exhibit at the Canadian War Museum.

Logistics soldiers must be tough, physically fit soldiers who can turn a wrench or wield a rifle as infantry with equal proficiency. The cultural line between combat arms and combat service support, part of a class distinction as old as Canada's army, must be dissolved. If we are to survive on this battlefield, the supporting and the supported, more than ever before, need to be more like each other.

10

A Hard About Turn

After we go to Kandahar, nobody will be accusing us of not stepping to the plate. Going down there takes some political guts, because we will likely take casualties.

— Captain Angus Matheson, in Adnan R. Khan,
"We Will Likely Take Casualties," *Maclean's*[77]

Paddy Earles and I arrived in Theatre on 11 February near the front of the task force airflow. Two days before we touched down at KAF on 9 February 2006, a LAV III from the battle group's Alpha Company, the company with the nickname "Red Devils," struck an IED in northern Kandahar Province. It happened during the mission rehearsal training being run for the Patricias by the U.S. Task Force Gun Devil. The assumption of the reins in Kandahar by the Canadian task force was still three weeks away. Fortunately no soldiers were killed in this contact. Hope and his Patricias had been on the ground for nearly two weeks and inserting some of our logistics troops this early in the personnel airflow had been a real uphill battle. The brigade staff planners had wanted bayonets on the ground first. The loggies could come at the end after the operators were squared away. The NSE we were replacing did not have the same projection capability mine had, and combat service support was needed immediately to support the battle group's mission rehearsal training well beyond the wire of KAF. We lobbied the commander hard to get at least some of the soldiers of the NSE in country early but without the support of the battle group I think I would have lost this argument.

The first issue that confronted us was a dramatic change in the agreed concept of battle group operations as worked out between Lieutenant-Colonel Hope and myself at the Green Beans Coffee Shop on KAF in the late summer of 2005. We had caught a whisper of this at Camp Mirage on 9 February as we approached the last leg of our journey north into Afghanistan:

> The PPCLI is going to stay off KAF in its entirety all of the time. There will not be an entire LAV company left on KAF for refit — ever. New Forward Operating Bases would need to be constructed, et cetera, et cetera.

Rumour and innuendo tend to swirl around Camp Mirage like vicious dust devils. Tales of what is happening "up north" in the sands of Kandahar can prey on the mind only to evaporate on arrival at KAF, so I did not put much credence into what I was hearing. In this case the rumours turned out to be absolutely true. The notion of the LAV companies of Task Force Orion conducting operations up to and including combat for periods of five to seven days' duration was indeed scrapped.[78] It was already clear at this point in early February that we would need all the infantry all the time. Furthermore, and most crippling to my support concept given the premium requirement for infantry, there was no scope for an entire LAV company to retool at KAF while the other two conducted operations, as was the original intent. Intellectually, I could understand the need for the shift. The small size of the Canadian logistics battalion however, would be felt more acutely with this dramatic shift in plan. I was not sure we could in fact sustain the new plan. Hell, I was still worried about having the right numbers to support the original operating concept that was markedly easier to support. The change in concept made eminent tactical sense but reshaping the logistics battalion to support this dramatic manoeuvre change would be akin to steering RMS *Titanic* an hour after the iceberg collision.

The battlefield upon which this concept of operations would be executed is one our grandfathers would not well recognize. I have been on scores of battlefield tours and memorized details and figures inside

National Park Service and Parks Canada interpretation centres. There is nothing in this experience that lends weight to a description of the contemporary battlefield in Kandahar. Different models come close, so I propose to start with them.

One concept that has worked well for me in the training and preparation of officers and soldiers is centred on those funky lava lamps from the 1960s with their floating blobs of wax inside an oil medium. When the lamp is turned on, the wax melts and forms irregular shapes and blobs. These blobs represent the defended enclosures like KAF and the smaller FOBs we maintain beyond the major bases. The oil medium represents all the long stretches of Kandahar Province in between our forward operating bases. When you are in the oil, you might as well be at the base of Vimy Ridge looking up, for this is the no man's land of our generation. It is exactly what the glance over the parapet looks like in the age of irregular warfare. In this battle, there is an omnipresent weight of uncertainty that comes from the knowledge that the enemy will attack

This photo was taken just off the Tarin Kot Highway. When we scuttled the original operating concept and decided to operate out of decentralized FOBs, the logistics unit had to hit the road much more than we had planned. Moving to FOBs and operating off KAF was the right thing to do. However, the change in concept made the pressures on a small logistics unit acute.

only at the time and place of his choosing. The lava lamp model was all the rage with the doctrine writers of the 1990s who were trying to get a handle on the future battlefield.

Another analogy that might help to convey the reality of the ground is to think of the non-contiguous battle space as a highly polished walnut table upon which little droplets of water are scattered. Participating in U.S. Army convoy lanes at Fort Lee, Virginia, in February 2005 and watching how American truck convoys were aggressively protected between FOBs, I was reminded of a grand old walnut table my grandmother owned. This table had so many coats of polish and elbow grease burnished into it over years of cherished use that the surface glistened like a brand new Buick. Of course, when you spilled liquid on the table it formed many little pools or droplets arranged in random patterns. The droplets of water in this model, represent our defended enclosures, either major bases or FOBs. The burnished walnut between the water droplets is our no man's land, in any direction you move. In the contemporary operating environment with no definable front and rear area, the flow of supplies along a progressively more dangerous line as it was in the Second World War is neither realistic nor possible. You cannot get the feel of this modern battlefield by peeking at a map or making a helicopter tour. Visitors who came into the theatre and flew everywhere could easily walk away with the wrong impression. Small distances take a long time to cover on the ground. An 80-kilometre road trip in an escorted convoy can easily take 16 hours because of IED threats, vehicle breakdowns, or both.

I listen closely to Mohammed Arif's assessment of an insurgent attack in mid-June on the fringes of Kandahar City. My own convoy would be rolling right past the point on Highway 1 where this horrific attack took place. This is the reality of this kind of warfare. The non-contiguous battlefield is also typified by the absence of battle. A segment of road can be as peaceful and alluring as a Muskoka cottage lane. Then, in an unforgettable moment, the same pastoral vista can erupt into a ball of chaos — intense explosion, small-arms fire, and section-level drills where the soldier finds himself in the fight of his life. An hour later the violence and the noise abate, and serenity returns so abruptly that you have trouble believing that it happened at all. No more chateau headquarters on the drive out of Normandy. No more luxury of always having a defined assembly area leading to an attack position with a clear and definite idea of where your enemy is. This level of certainty has evaporated from the contemporary battlefield we face in Afghanistan. Mohammed Arif's description of the affected part of the highway speaks to the calm after the storm, a perfectly fit road for travel. The violence of the lava lamp battlefield has again evaporated. The hope and determination in Mohammed Arif's voice strike me as typical of many Afghans I have spoken to who are tired of decades of war and wish to make their country into a stable Islamic republic. I think long and hard on Mohammed Arif's optimism and national pride as we mount up in our armoured Mercedes G-Wagon and flow into town with the convoy. As we pull over at the outer lip of KAF to charge our weapons it occurs to me that if we really want to know how Canada is doing in Afghanistan, we should ask the Afghans more often.

The battlefields of our grandfathers and fathers were lethal but linear in their layout. They could be etched out on stiff collage-cloth models with neat straight lines and discussed with an almost reassuring mathematical predictability. In fact, a theatre of operations could be plotted with such certainty that it could be divided in half right off the bat into a forward combat zone and a communication zone right behind it. At the extreme forward edge of the combat zone was the tangible knife edge of enemy contact known as the front or forward edge of the battle area (FEBA). The FEBA was where the bulk of combat occurred; the veritable source of the thunder. It was at this edge that our army fought in two world wars, relying on the British army to furnish the army level support organizations in the communication zone.[79] The farther one moved back from the FEBA toward the communications zone, the farther the soldier was removed from the thunder and, for the most part, the safer he became. A paradigm like this has limited application in southern Afghanistan where the front erupts where and when the insurgents chose to make it erupt.

The FEBA for a logistics convoy was all around it because the Taliban chose where and when they would hit our convoys. These attacks, along with the difficult climate and geography of Afghanistan, are defining characteristics of this new battlefield.

FOB MARTELLO

The revised concept of operations called for the three LAV III companies to operate all the time from forward operating bases. FOB Martello is a great Canadian story. FOB Martello was to be built out of the side of a mountain in the Shah Wali Kot District of Kandahar Province. The terrain in Shah Wali Kot has little to recommend it. The landscape looks much like the surface of the moon with rock and sand and everywhere those thin "pie crust–style" mountains. The little Canadian outpost along the Tarin Kot Highway had a tactical purpose but also a low key strategic one. For Ian Hope, the FOB had excellent tactical value. Martello would be home to the bulk of Alpha Company. The position unsettled the village of El Bak; it was like a chicken bone lodged in the throat of the pro-Taliban community. The implication for one of our few allies in the south was even greater. Martello became a valuable way station for Dutch forces as they moved north into their operational area in Uruzgan. The Dutch leaned mightily on FOB Martello as they began their series of long road moves in May.

The site for FOB Martello was immediately adjacent to the Tarin Kot Highway and smack dab in the middle of a number of less established but highly travelled Taliban pathways. As brilliant as the tactical placement of Martello was, it was bleak from the perspective of engineering and logistics. The construction of this FOB became our biggest effort throughout the months of April and May. This effort from a logistic standpoint was led by Scott McKenzie, my deputy commanding officer. McKenzie is a British Columbia boy and fine example of the modern warrior poet, a devout rugby player, hunter, and book aficionado. As an officer in the Electrical Mechanical Engineering Branch of the army he has already completed his master's degree and logged one valuable tour of duty at National Defence headquarters in Ottawa. For a young major, Scott knew the Ottawa waters well — particularly where equipment and engineering were concerned. He knew which levers to pull to get attention. I have spent most of my career in the field and have never served at the Ottawa headquarters, so having Scott as part of my team in Kandahar was extremely fortunate. He was ferocious and tactful in gleaning engineering solutions to our equipment problems in southern Afghanistan. Scott commanded the unit while I was at home and he had done the initial FOB Martello reconnaissance for the first couple of sites with Kirk Gallinger, Alpha Company commander. The initial reports on requirements were bleak from the logistics perspective. A great deal of engineering and CSS support was required to develop it to the point that it was defendable and sustainable for Alpha Company.

Construction of the most northern FOB commenced on 15 April 2006. The NSE maintained a permanent detachment in the FOB to provide the echelon for Alpha Company soldiers in the location. Additionally, we sent sustainment convoys every two or three days to build up the required engineer and logistic stores to support the construction plan. Martello lay at the intersection of a number of insurgent traffic lines or "rat lines." The pro-Taliban village of El Bak could be watched from the FOB's perch. FOB Martello for me demonstrated Canadian resolve. It took a lot of hard work and courage to get it built in such forlorn topography, but it was a physical manifestation of Canada's commitment to come here and do meaningful work. We were not going to knit sweaters on the airbase; instead our infantry were out and living at the grassroots municipal level. Martello's other great purpose was born out of its proximity to the Tarin Kot Highway. Tarin Kot was the road that Dutch forces used to deploy from Kandahar into their operational area — Uruzgan Province. Martello served as a friendly safe haven for the many Dutch convoys that were needed to set up the Dutch task force in the summer of 2006. On 10 June 2006, FOB Martello was opened officially. I went to the official opening with Pat Earles, on a CH-147 Chinook helicopter. Alpha Company hosted a *shura* at the FOB that day and General Fraser sat in the inner sanctum with the elders of the province and the district. Besides supporting FOB Martello, the NSE continued to support the Gumbad Platoon House. This area grew increasingly more dangerous for ground-based convoys as the tour went on, and the terrain was particularly difficult for heavy CSS vehicles to manoeuvre through.

PATROL BASE WILSON

Patrol Base Wilson was home to Major Nick Grimshaw's Bravo Company headquarters and one of his platoons. The Patrol Base was co-located with the Zhari District Centre. It was located some 25 kilometres west of Kandahar City perched north of the Arghandab River and the Panjwayi District where some 2,000 Taliban warriors had been massing for the months of June and July 2006. Grimshaw was almost always under fire at Patrol Base Wilson, and he carefully watched the progress of the Taliban buildup along the Arghandab River to his south like a patient high schooler might observe a science experiment. Gathering intelligence and taking notes and observations from conversation with the local populace, he put together a disturbing jigsaw puzzle of a large concentration of enemy. Kandahar City was to be returned to Taliban control by the end of July and if Kandahar Province was a bomb, Nick Grimshaw's company sat perpetually on its fuse. It was not unusual for our convoys to get attacked when replenishing Bravo Company. The NSE columns that sustained his group always went with extra G-Wagon doors to swap out the doors that had been rocketed.

FOB SPIN BOLDAK

In the last week in June, I took my first trip south to Spin Boldak. The trip was necessary to ensure the camp was ready to receive Charlie Company of the PPCLI for occupation in July 2006. Highway 4 is the road we take Spin Boldak, the border town between Afghanistan and Pakistan. If you continue on the road into Pakistan you will eventually reach Quetta and Karachi beyond. I watched a parade of dust devils in the open fields along the road. These swirls of dirt look like miniature tornadoes and they jump and skip with an organic dexterity. The dust devils had the irrational effect of making you feel less alone in the Afghanistan country-side. They seemed like friendly spirits to me. They are widespread, haunt-ing, and comforting at the same time, an alien presence that assures you that you are never alone. The site on arrival at the camp was not what we expected. The French soldiers, who had occupied the American camp with an MP platoon from the 101st Airborne Division, were in the act of gutting the infrastructure and sending it to their new location in Jalal-abad. The American captain who commanded the military police was delighted at the prospect of Canadians moving in. He could not contain his pleasure as the chief cook outlined his proposals for the fresh ration kitchen. My rusty Canadian French was given a workout while I tried to be tactful about keeping the equipment there. It is one thing to move from your house but quite another to strip out the panelling and air con-ditioners as you leave. The French were being ungracious, because they were concerned that their new quarters in Jalalabad would lack many of the comforts Spin Boldak offered. They reminded me of squirrels back home grabbing on to any and everything to see them through a barren season. I was not going to let them leave with Charlie Company com-mander, Major Bill Fletcher's infrastructure. Fortunately for my cause, we had a U.S. Special Forces sergeant-major with us who knew what the camp had before the French occupied it. He was instrumental in stop-ping the gutting of quarters and loss of basic infrastructure.

Once settled in the camp, I found it had a certain Old Fort Henry, Santa Fe feel to it. We worked to furnish it with enough services to keep Charlie Company comfortable. I often wonder how the French garrison made out in Jalalabad.

The area of operation around Spin Boldak had previously been a French Special Forces responsibility. Major Bill Fletcher and his Charlie Company was replacing them. Taking over the reins at Spin Boldak was a completely different suite of challenges from those presented by Martello. Martello was a pile of rocks and sand when we started and it demanded a ton of engineer work. Spin Boldak was a well-established FOB complete with an Afghan work force of some 40 local employees. Several reconnais-sance trips were conducted, one of which I attended with Warrant Officer

Turner, Bill Fletcher's company quartermaster sergeant, the senior soldier NCO who was in charge of intimate logistic support to the company. This also served as a good initial ground reconnaissance for Force Protection Platoon, my own convoy escort infantry gang. The road to Spin Boldak was an ironic blend of superior pavement for the first 40 kilometres and punishing, poor quality road way for the last 35. The sudden and dramatic change in road quality conveyed the distinct impression that the construction of this road was a project that had run out of funding. President Daoust had played both ends against the middle in attracting Soviet and U.S. investment in Afghanistan infrastructure. The first 45 kilometres of Highway 4 comprise a project where money found its intended target. The remaining 50-odd kilometres to the Pakistan border are atrociously rough. Highway 4 was shockingly narrow, perhaps its most defining characteristic.

Beginning on 2 July 2006, Task Force Orion began the occupation of FOB Spin Boldak. This FOB was well developed, but I elected to beef up Fletcher's Charlie Company with a section of support soldiers from the NSE to assist with support in the early days of occupation. Captain Bobby Alolega, the Supply Platoon Commander headed up this support for the first week in Spin Boldak. The support arrangement in Spin Boldak is based on the hiring of experienced local Afghan employees, contracted services, and a small nucleus of cooks, mechanics, and truckers from the NSE.

REALITY HURTS!

Having all these FOBs under the revised operating concept meant more convoys to more places over dangerous ground. In an area of operations where routine movement is a combat operation, it was not surprising that we met the enemy early in the tour. Indeed the weight of enemy activity was felt immediately during our vehicle movement between these various defended FOBs. Our convoys into Kandahar were ambushed on a number of occasions on their way to the PRT site, Camp Nathan Smith. We had prepared the soldiers for this kind of fighting but the realization that they were in it even before our Transfer of Authority (TOA) date of 1 March 2006 was somewhat disconcerting. I recall one of my corporals going on his first convoy on 28 February and emptying nearly a complete magazine of 5.56 mm into a machine gun position during a sophisticated ambush. The convoy escaped without human or vehicle casualties but the corporal, a military truck driver, was pretty charged up.

Another view of the FOB guns.

In preparing a logistics unit, whether it is a battalion or a section, the dominant factor in its design will be the operational concept of the supported force. Most of your choices for a logistics plan tend to follow one of two paths: centralized or decentralized. If you are a small logistics unit (as we were) you are wise to opt for a centralized support structure, like our original plan to support three LAV companies from one base — using KAF as the main logistics node. A decentralized concept with FOBs all over the province makes an already small unit downright brittle. By the time all three company FOBs were occupied and running on 2 July 2006, logistically speaking we were at our weakest point. When July exploded with combat activity with the Canadian battle group operating in two different Afghan provinces, the NSE was already sucking on fumes.

The new operating concept was clever, in the respect that it put Canadian soldiers out living with the Afghans all the time. It is difficult to get a feel for municipal subtleties so necessary to operating effectively in Afghanistan when you roar out with your force and then return to KAF in a day or two. Indeed a FOB is a useful way of operating on a lava lamp battlefield. However, there are trade-offs when you build them. First, you must use some of your soldiers to guard them, and if they are guarding, they cannot be beyond the wire patrolling. Using FOBs to base operations was the right thing to do tactically; however, for long periods of June and July 2006 we could barely sustain them.

FOBs and secured points on the ground had to be sustained far from KAF. There would be no returning to the base for major logistics overhauls.

Make no mistake about it, what defined Canadian operations during the course of our tour from March to August 2006 was the fact that 1 PPCLI went out and lived in the communities, the hills, and villages with the Kandahar population. They fought and lived beyond the secure confines of KAF for the entire duration with many soldiers counting the number of showers they had in Afghanistan on one hand. The infantry would circle the LAVs and bed down in one spot in the evening, and by morning be in a completely different district, scores of kilometres away. The agility of the infantry required flexible logistics and we strove to provide just that. An agile battle group played on the mind of our enemy. However, to say the change in concept created challenges for the NSE is a gross understatement. The changed operating concept should have broken us. At the risk of sounding bookish, I can only think that such a dramatic alteration in concept would have been forbidden in an outfit that was more in tune with professional logistics. The full up, all LAV companies operating off KAF all the time created immediately an air of quiet desperation for the members of my operations staff and line platoons who plied the Afghan countryside with Task Force Orion. For the entire tour, all 300 of us would be going flat out to keep this brave new plan afloat. On the other hand, I admired so much how the new plan reflected on Canadian resolve. Putting FOBs right in the throat of the enemy's communication lines and staying in the villages and countryside to get a good feel for what was really going on were vitally necessary steps to operating successfully in the complex battle space known as Kandahar. Here we were doing the job in a courageous and sound new way. A Canadian way. The logistics troops on the roads beyond the wire understood the gravity of what was at stake. They could read with accuracy how serious in particular the support situation had become in July during the peak of Canadian combat operations, and they refused to let the lines of communication snap. The tiny logistics unit that could — we 300 — had survived, at least for now, a very hard about turn.

Hello, we are from Canada. We are here to help ... and by the way, we are staying among you for a long, long time. Take the hand we are offering. It is genuine.

PART

3

11

King of the FOBs

30 June 2006. Tonight was a close one. Rocket attack on the main Dining Facility at KAF — eight wounded. One Canadian Corporal hanging by a thread.... We are all praying hard for him. He only arrived in country this week. A reservist. A young, young man.
— Lieutenant-Colonel John Conrad,
Kandahar Diary, June 2006

For heaven's sake, they were only stopping for bread. In the early hours of 15 June 2006, the netherworld between initial waking and full consciousness, a fully loaded civilian bus made its routine stop. The short halt was to enable a large busload of commuter passengers to purchase their lunchtime meal. The commuters were Afghan workers moving out from Kandahar to the KAF, the king of the south's forward operating bases some 18 kilometres away to begin the workday. Naan, an Afghan flat bread, offers a myriad of delights that elevates it well beyond the status of a mere staple, and I imagine that the routine selection of their lunch was one of but a few daily moments truly owned by these quiet, dignified men. It would be their last moment of domestic independence. The bomb went off shortly after they climbed back aboard the bus. The violence unfolded in the shadow of the Golden Arches, a well-known navigational feature near the eastern lip of the city. Golden Arches is the soldier's humorous term for the ramshackle structure over Highway 1 as you enter Kandahar City. The structure marks the western boundary of "IED Alley," a popular spot for IED strikes against us. Painted in a flat, fish-scale green, the arches are only vaguely reminiscent of the golden arches of McDonald's fast-food franchises, lending some insight into the creativity of the soldier who gave it its nickname. A Taliban operator took advantage of the mundane pattern of the commuters and placed the explosive on the bus. Fourteen of our Afghan employees were killed in the blast. In Kandahar, habits and patterns of behaviour are all too often the harbingers of violent death.

My heart goes out to the dead. I envision them shopping for their last lunch, peering into familiar ramshackle stalls that serve as shops, nodding greetings to familiar faces, all the while functioning on that human auto-pilot mode associated with the early morning. They are no different from the Canadian commuter who finds himself in the Tim Hortons drive-through line at 0645, waiting for a double-double and a toasted sesame seed bagel with cream cheese but not really recalling how the car came to be in the lineup or when he left his house. There are approximately 120 Afghan civilians who work for me supporting Canadian infrastructure on KAF, and I admire every one of them. They are bold enough to work for Canada on the big NATO base in the volatile Kandahar Province. They are strong enough to believe that stability and peace can be earned back in Kandahar. If our roles were reversed, I would like to believe I would have their courage to step forward. I have been asked by one of the senior Afghan supervisors if I can provide letters of condolence to the families so they can be used as part of a memorial shrine to the dead workers in their respective mosques. I am only too happy to comply, and I consult with my friend, Mohammed Arif, who tends to the daily cleaning of our buildings, to make sure I hit the right note with the letters. Mohammed Arif is a man I have grown to respect and like over the course of many conversations. I have told him about life in Canada and the similarities in certain aspects between his Hindu Kush Mountains and our own Rocky Mountains. I tell him how impressed I am with Afghanistan's raw beauty. He seems surprised that someone other than an Afghan can see beauty and value in his country — a telling glimpse into Afghanistan's national self-esteem. He is undeniably proud of this rugged natural beauty and makes no efforts to hide it.

The soft opening of Tim Hortons on 28 June 2006. Two days before the rocket attack on KAF that nearly claimed the life of a young Canadian soldier, four of us enjoy an advance coffee. From the left: Chief Warrant Officer Ramsay, Colonel Tom Putt, myself, and Major Mark Penney. The psychological boost that Timmies brought to the troops was immense and immediate.

His wide, moonlike face today is lined with worry. He gives me all the advice I need, but the words that strike me the most are his comments about the Taliban campaign season.

"June and July are always the bad months, sir," he tells me. "The violence will taper off next month and more again in September and things will be better again."

The comment has the timbre of a seasonal weather warning in Canada. I remember growing up on the farm being mindful that May to September were the months for tornadoes in southwestern Ontario. The habit of violence in Afghanistan is so undiscerning, so well ingrained that it has become as predictable to its people as the seasons. Life should not be lived this way regardless of race, religion, or creed. Mothers and fathers should not be so stoically capable of harvesting their dead children in the aftermath of a suicide attack. Men should not need to look forward to an "off season" where they can steal a break from violent death while they shop for bread.

On a battlefield marked by secured little pockets, KAF is the largest and most important. For us, KAF is our Gibraltar, our Boulogne in southern Afghanistan, our safest place, the king and sustainer of all of our FOBs. To the people of Kandahar Province, KAF must look like an enormous flying saucer that has landed on their planet from some distant point in the cosmos, with all the modern heavy equipment, fighting machines, and Western-style consumer goods and fast-food outlets ranging from Pizza Hut to Tim Hortons. The king of the FOBs must cut a pretty unusual groove in the antique city of Kandahar. For the Afghan workers, who must always keep an eye on fickle perceptions and the loyalties to tribe and family, KAF can be the most dangerous place they could possibly put themselves. To these men and the other brave Afghans like them, KAF must look like some sort of magic portal, through which they can salvage the future of their own country. It takes guts for them to work here.

Our warriors joke about KAF. The base is much maligned for its security and association with safety, comfort, and amenities. We never lost sight of the fact however that the protection of KAF was our highest priority. There are virtually no armies in the long reach of history that have not had to pay attention to their logistics heartland. Catering to the security of your lines of supply must be done if you hope to be successful. As Richard M. McMurray has so eloquently stated in his entertaining study of the armies of Northern Virginia and Tennessee, "All armies have to defend their sources of supply, and sometimes their operations are shaped by the need to do so."[80] Without KAF there can be no operation. The security of our military operation begins right at this gigantic NATO base. Nothing reinforces this point as much for me as the endless day of 30 June 2006. It was the day I stopped keeping track of attacks on the airbase. The big division operation, Operation Mountain Thrust, was in its earliest stages — what we in the army call preliminary moves and we were also preparing to host a modest Canada Day celebration on the camp. The big event for Canada Day was to be the opening of the new Tim Hortons store on KAF. I had spent most of the morning in briefings and preparations with the Tim's crew and preparing some notes for General Fraser, who was to do the official opening. We had had a recovery convoy out for most of the day assisting 1 PPCLI with some vehicle repairs and extractions out of contact with the Taliban. The column had broken down shy of the camp as dusk was falling, and I stopped by to check on their day and get the latest news from the Tarin Kot Highway, the northern route they had travelled. About an hour later, my driver, Master Corporal Shawn Crowder and I, were in the Main Dining Facility at KAF. We almost always permit ourselves a dessert at night and the question, "Shall we have a dessert?" is generally rhetorical. That night I remember being mildly shocked when Crowder said no.

"Don't feel like one," he mumbled tiredly. The Tim Hortons store had opened unofficially two days earlier in the act of what the Timmies officials called a "soft opening" and was still a novelty. It would be impossible to overstate the positive effect the new Tim Hortons store had on our collective morale. And the joy was shared by more than just Canadians. The American, Dutch, and British soldiers could all be found in the long queue outside the coffee shop in the morning. A number of franchises already existed on KAF including a Burger King and a Pizza Hut. They served products that were tasty and a definite change from the routine mess food but there would be no mistaking them for the real franchises in North America. The Tim Hortons store, however, was not just another pale surrogate. It was the real deal. An unofficial soft opening of the franchise occurred on 29 June 2006, and it was highly successful. When we walked into the franchise, it was like being back in Canada for a few moments. A tastefully framed burlap coffee bag adorned one of the walls. Over the counter was a plasma screen television advertising both meal specials that could be mopped up with your KAF paper coins and the Tim Hortons franchise history. The illusion was powerful and reassuring. It was Canadian soil right down to the familiar logo on a hot double-double.

Tim Hortons inside the Canadian Forces falls under the auspices of the Canadian Forces Personnel Support Agency (CFPSA). In Kandahar the store came under the control of the NSE as a logistics amenity. On 30 June, Major-General Doug Langdon, the man in charge of the

Tim Hortons Canada Day Opening. From the left: myself, Major-General Doug Langdon, and Colonel Tom Putt.

Canadian Forces Personnel Support Agency, was in country to oversee the historic event. General Langdon, a Canadian air force officer who had commanded the base in Gander, Newfoundland earlier in his career, was an enormously pleasant surprise. His visit to Kandahar for the Tim Hortons opening was one we were not looking forward to. Any senior guests from the Ottawa headquarters had the potential to bring more work for you when they arrived. Not the case with Langdon, who had a most unassuming style. Rather than present himself as a VIP guest and a small tax on our meagre hosting resources, he pitched in to help with myriad sundry events and chores up to and including serving beer to our soldiers with the rest of the CFPSA civilian employees. His grounded, simple style set me to thinking about General Byng's robust farmer approach to leading his corps in the First World War.

"Why don't we go over to Tim's and have a coffee?" I suggested.

Shawn Crowder didn't drink coffee, but the thought of trying something new and deeply familiar stirred his interest. Off we went. Ten minutes later, familiar-smelling coffee in hand and feeling smug, we were on the way back toward the mess tent.

Whooooosh! Bang!

A 107 mm rocket crash caused us to jump. The projectile had impacted right in front of us between two wings of the tented main dining facility we had vacated only a score of minutes before. Scott McKenzie, my deputy, was walking in the opposite direction and out of my line of sight. He recalled the moment as well:

> That attack was the closest I have seen. I had just stepped out of the building I work in to head back to my tent when I heard the first impact, which sounded really close. Then I heard a long drawn out whine of the next incoming round (the longer you hear the whine, the closer it likely is). I looked up and saw the second rocket streak past and impact behind the main kitchen that was about 200 metres from where I was standing. Too close for comfort to tell you the truth ...
>
> — Major Scott McKenzie, "Afghanistan Updates"

The haunting, all-too-familiar wail of the KAF attack siren went off and we parted company. Crowder headed for the tent line bunkers, and I hot-footed to the battalion headquarters to get a better feel for what had happened. I checked in at the command post and got a quick brief from the duty officer. Our recovery convoy had made it back onto the camp and were out of danger. My infantry soldiers guarding the ammunition section on the far side of the field had heard the rockets coming overhead, but they were unscathed and safe in their own little bunker at the ammunition point that the RSM had orchestrated.

I made my way over to the smoke-filled dining facility to see for myself what had occurred. The voices of stricken soldiers varied from screams to moans inside the burning mess tent. Colonel Tom Putt, the task force deputy commander, was there, as was Ian Hope, and I gave Tom a cursory report on how the NSE had fared in the attack — so far it appeared that no one in my unit was hurt but this could only be confirmed once the painstaking head count was completed and all sections had called in to the command post.

After every rocket attack, we had to account for every soldier one by one. The confirmation of names and sections inside the unit was recorded on a large board like the ones used in bingo games. It was a perverse board game to play in the wee hours when the attacks usually occurred. It normally took about 15 minutes to fill the board and determine if someone remained unaccounted for. I was sure there were Canadians in the mess tent because we had stopped to chat to a small group as we left on our Tim Hortons run. The KAF Quick Reaction Force under the guidance of an officer from the Royal Air Force Air Field Defence Squadron was controlling the scene at the dining facility. Soldiers were starting to be hauled out on stretchers, and I peered anxiously at each of them to get a feel for severity of the injuries and determine if any of the soldiers were mine.

Indeed, eight Canadians were injured that night. In the case of Master Bombardier Bounyarat Makthepharak, the injury was nearly fatal as some of the shrapnel from the rocket had punctured his chest. Makthepharak, a popular soldier, hadn't even adjusted to the Afghan time zone. He had only been in theatre a week, but his war was over. General Fraser told me later that when he went to visit the injured Canadian in the KAF hospital, he noted that the surgeon had Makthepharak's chest cavity opened "like a '57 Chevy." The 107 mm shrapnel had passed close to his heart, and the resulting wound had necessitated some courageous surgery to save his life. Performing a miracle a day was routine at the sterling Canadian-led Role 3 hospital. Every one of the men and women of the medical corps who worked in this remarkable unit were walking, talking heroes. It would be impossible to describe even the edges of the large body of phenomenal work these medical people did, but the preservation of this young master bombardier is one that stands out like an exclamation mark.

It is funny. Since I have come back from southern Afghanistan, my dreams about Kandahar and the king of the FOBs are frequent, but while I was there I rarely had dreams. I would normally stumble back to my tent and collapse in a heap until either rocket drills or Paddy's cheery goddamn alarm clock woke us both for the next day. That day, 30 June, was an exception. In the earliest hours of Canada Day, while Master Bombardier Makthepharak fought to stay alive on the other side of the camp, I checked in at NSE headquarters one last time to make sure everyone including the duty staff was all right. I lumbered back toward my tent as unsteadily as the wounded American Civil War soldier in Stephen Crane's *The Red Badge of Courage*. I stopped one last time to ensure all was good with the Tim Hortons group, so eagerly poised for the sunrise and their highly anticipated grand opening on 1 July, now hours away.

The Timmies personnel weren't too badly rattled by the rocket attack, so I continued to walk toward my tent feeling a thousand years old. I found my cot in the dark and sat quietly for a bit, giving a wordless thanks to Providence for steering me away from the dessert table in the dining facility. At some point I fell asleep in full, sweat-dried uniform, service pistol, boots, and all. It was the deepest sleep I have ever known, almost biblical in its quality, and inside it I had the strangest dream. I was fighting to get through a ferocious driving rainstorm in the G-Wagon, or it might have been my command post Bison. In any case it was wicked, world-ending weather with thunder and flash floods and driving rain. I made it to a house that ended up being the old yellow brick farmhouse in Wallace Township where I had grown up in southwestern Ontario. When I got to the farmhouse, my Grandmother Alice, who passed away in 1996, came out onto the verandah and immediately began to hug me. She was saying something and kept earnestly repeating it, but I couldn't make sense of her words. She held on to me tighter and tighter and wouldn't let go. I couldn't draw a breath, her grasp was so tight!

I woke up in a panic to shake this crushing feeling and saw immediately that I wasn't back in Wallace Township with Grandma but rather in my Weatherhaven tent at KAF. It was after four in the morning, and I was awash in an inexplicable sense of melancholy and loss. I was extremely close to my grandmother. She had virtually raised me while my parents both worked off that Wallace Township farm. She came to the VIA Rail Station in Kitchener the day I left for basic training in July 1983, the last time that I really talked with her in any detail. I haven't dreamed of her since her death in 1996, at least no dream that I ever could recall after waking. It was the most realistic dream I have ever known, and it was hard to have it all tucked neatly away in the recesses of my mind for 0730 when again I presented myself back to the living world at KAF and our modest 1 July celebrations.

> Whenever a coalition soldier is killed in action, an event called a ramp ceremony takes place. This was my first occasion to attend one ... In this ceremony troops of all the nations on KAF move out in formation to the airfield and conduct a short parade while the bodies of those killed in action are loaded onto an aircraft for the return home. It was actually a pretty moving experience. It was not the kind of rah rah ceremony that we frequently associate with the Americans, it was sombre, simple, and extremely powerful. We lined up on the tarmac along with Dutch, U.K., Romanian, Australian, and U.S. soldiers.
>
> — Major Scott McKenzie, "Afghanistan Updates"

KAF is best known to the average Canadian for the ramp ceremonies that are sometimes televised from Kandahar by the major networks. The attention of the entire airfield community tightens together for the ramp ceremonies that are normally held in the craziest of hours — late night or pre-dawn to suit the demands of the air transport schedules of the different NATO nations. The attention of the public is sharpened for combat deaths and the soldiers who are killed in Afghanistan continue to have an enormous impact on the average Canadian. Lisa LaFlamme of CTV interviewed me in March at the Canadian headquarters right after one of our earliest ramp ceremonies on the tour, the one for Corporal Paul Davis. The feelings that swirled inside me as his casket went by were complex and focused on my own youth. Looking over the top of Davis's casket, I let my mind drift back to a happier time with my own family — getting sunburned and tired out in the beautiful sapphire water of Lake Huron on a perfect July afternoon; stopping for Chinese food in Hanover with my parents at the end of that endless summer day and feeling tired,

secure, and happy underneath the sunburn. How many days had Paul
Davis enjoyed like that? Would his parents and spouse be thinking of
those cherished sun-warmed Canadian afternoons as well? How heavy is
their burden? Do they know that every Canadian soldier in Afghanistan,
every soldier on this FOB will carry a little piece of this weight for them?

The word that my mind stops on as the casket is set down on the
Hercules flight deck with the finality of an aluminum clang is *family*.
Family. The fallen aren't colleagues. In a fighting organization a fallen
soldier is a part of your family and cap badges are meaningless. Our
soldiers in Kandahar operate in a different sort of world from the one
we appreciate here at home. Neither of these worlds is less real than the
other but they are markedly different. The repatriation of a dead soldier
is the one time when the two worlds intersect; when KAF and Trenton,
Ontario, stand side by side in the Canadian conscience. Through the
keyhole of a soldier's repatriation the public is given a glimpse into the
price of the war.

*Cutting the ribbon on 1 July 2006. From the left: Major-General Doug Langdon, Doug
Anthony of Tim Hortons, a wounded solder, and Brigadier-General David Fraser.*

KAF was to Canada's Task Force Afghanistan what Boulogne had been to the Canadian Corps in the First World War, and what the early Mulberry harbour at Arromarche meant to the Canadians who came ashore on Juno Beach on D-Day in the Second World War — our major operational supply base. However, getting the correct volumes of *matériel* into KAF was only the beginning of the logistic challenge, and it was, in truth, the easiest leg of the journey. KAF was only a way station for *matériel*. Forward delivery beyond the wire is a combat operation each and every time.

12

Kandahar Overdrive

Some things you have to live with: the split decisions that you make and their spider webs of inherent repercussion, the wounds you receive and those you inflict on your enemy. The unforgivable insults to humanity your senses can't avoid in the heart of a war, in the centre of a fight. You must live with these things as a soldier and as a human being.

— Lieutenant-Colonel John Conrad,
Kandahar Diary, July 2006

We departed nearly on time in the pre-dawn hours of 22 July 2006, and the powerful sense of a fate foreshadowed whispered by me undetected. I should have noticed the irregularity in the fabric of the day. Convoys almost never departed on time from KAF. There was always a last-minute equipment malfunction — a vehicle that blew a tire or a radio that winkled out — that prevented a punctual departure. The day earmarked for the triumphant return of Task Force Orion from Helmand Province was 22 July 2006. The next 48 hours would galvanize into my most vivid memory from the tour, the days I replay in my mind's eye over and over again, with pieces of it that stand out in crystalline clarity — sights, smells, and remnants of conversation. The Task Force had operated together in Helmand Province, the operational area assigned to the United Kingdom, at distances that at times exceeded 350 kilometres. The battle group had performed magnificently and destroyed a number of Taliban. To bring them all the way back, the NSE needed to create a service station in the middle of nowhere to bridge the long gaps between the battle group location in the lower Helmand River Valley and KAF. This mini Canadian Tire store that we were hauling is called a commodity point in military jargon. The commodity point, once set up and defended, would replenish the battle group in Helmand and give them enough combat supplies to make it home to KAF. On the morning of 22 July, we left KAF at 0430 with the logistics vehicles to get the job done. The column had two Coyote escorts as well as three Bison armoured vehicles from both the NSE and 1 PPCLI — lots of escort firepower. On the western edge of Kandahar City, we were forced to halt to avoid a Taliban ambush that was unfolding to the west on some Afghanistan National Security Forces (ANSF). A platoon from Major Nick Grimshaw's Bravo Company came to the aid of the ANSF and smoothed things out. The logistics wagons were on the move to Helmand Province again by 0600. At 0800 we arrived at the planned location for the commodity point near the junction of Highway 1 and a route that I only knew as Secondary Road 611. Route 611 harboured more than just a little notoriety for the Canadians. Major Bill Fletcher had experienced so many IEDs on Route 611 when he had taken his Charlie Company up to the Sangin District in May that he stayed off it and drove his LAV IIIs along its side. The armoured vehicles, Coyotes and Bisons, took up perimeter security and the CSS trucks were centrally positioned.

The battle group began to arrive in platoon- and company-sized groups around 1100, the sound and dust cloud that telegraphed the leading edge of 1 PPCLI being detectable from a long way off. The first group in comprised of elements of Major Steve Gallagher's artillery battery dragging their prized U.S. Marine Corps 155 mm guns. The earth around us, so quiet for so long, exploded into a cacophony of noise and disciplined activity. It was a fascinating spectacle as chunk by chunk of the battle group lumbered into the commodity point. The scene smacked of a brontosaurus feeding frenzy; prehistoric-looking armoured vehicles and trucks waiting in line to get to the raw nourishment of the diesel pond. Boxes of food and cartons of water were hurled from logistics wagons to the infantry company quartermaster sergeants. Very few words were spoken between us. Very few were necessary. As the white-hot Afghan sun slowly passed its apex overhead, the collective sense of purpose and razor-sharp attention to time bonded every soldier in that commodity point together tighter than blood. The LAVs and trucks seemed to move slowly yet the complete replenishment took less than 30 minutes. After the last LAV III was filled with diesel, Lieutenant-Colonel Ian Hope gave a brief speech to the battle group about the operation they had just completed. Battle-weary but triumphant from 7–22 July, Task Force Orion had been in some 36 firefights with the Taliban, recovered nine ammunition caches, and seized narcotic product with a street value in the neighbourhood of $15 million. The operations had seen both Canadian and Afghan National Army soldiers hurt and one Canadian killed in action. There would be two more killed before we made it back. I spoke briefly with Ian Hope before we got on the road. I had lost one of two Coyote escorts to mechanical breakdown. The lethal-looking reconnaissance vehicle with its 25 mm cannon seemed to pout from its useless position on the back of our flatbed recovery trailer. Hope and I agreed to stick close in one large column as we made the long journey back to KAF.

Master Corporal Gorman, who had driven the big diesel 16-ton refueller out with us that morning, mentioned that the air conditioner was not working in the cab. He commented correctly that it would be a long ride back to KAF. Air conditioners are not luxuries in Kandahar. With the amount of protective gear our soldiers wear and the punishing temperatures, the air conditioning unit is a life-saving piece of gear. If at all possible, a truck will be pulled off the road when its air conditioner is broken. Since the air conditioning in the refueller had conked out during the trip this was not an option.

"Tell you what, Mr. Gorman, Crowder and I will swap you out. The G-Wagon air conditioner is working fine and you've been working harder than me today."

It was true that the refuellers had done a great job in the blistering heat, blasting diesel from their pressure nozzles into parched LAV III tanks. My God, it was hot in that cab. Shawn Crowder had put some 20 bottles of water in the cab to sustain us. Twenty minutes into the convoy we were sweat-soaked and breathing in little clips. Shawn was less than impressed with his CO for making the switch, but he said nothing about it. I, like a jackass, said the words that I will forever want back.

"Geez, it's hot in here, Crowder. Maybe we'll get hit and we can get some cooler air."

"I'm okay with the heat, sir," he retorted.

The ridiculous attempt to keep the mood light had prophetic weight. I wish I hadn't said anything.

Staying close to Ian's column worked for a while, but close is a relative term in a convoy that is 20-plus kilometres long. Just before 1700 one of our heavy logistics trucks broke down. We had to stop the logistics convoy to put the truck on the wrecker. Stopping at anytime in this country can mean trouble, and we work hard to make these necessary halts as short as possible. After crossing the Arghandab River on Kandahar's western edge, we had to make another brief stop to allow the mechanics to back off the brakes on the HLVW, which was being towed. The Arghandab River is a defining geographical feature in this newest corner of Canadian history. Alexander the Great once camped on its banks with an army of 30,000. Twenty-five kilometres west of Kandahar City, the river seemed to be an unofficial boundary between the nasty intensity of Panjwayi and Zhari Districts — the scene of many of our fights in 2006 — and Kandahar. Crossing the Arghandab from the west normally signified a return to the relative safety of the city. Not this time. We were back on the move again by 1715 and sometime within the next 15 minutes we were hit by a vehicle borne IED. A suicide bomber.

The attack was typical yet surreal — a small Toyota Hiace van slowly made its way along our convoy, travelling in the opposite direction on the north edge of the road. One moment I was dimly aware of the white cab over-style Toyota and the next moment there was an enormous explosion louder than anything I ever recall hearing and a large ball of smoke, body, and vehicle parts expanding toward our diesel truck. For a second I thought the enemy had missed and we were about to accelerate and get the hell out of there. Then, in the next fraction of a second, we noticed the Bison that had been to my front before the fireball was in the ditch. We immediately set up a security cordon. One of my Bisons fired off a three-round burst from its machine gun at some suspicious-looking bystanders who were observing the incident from the ditch with too much nonchalance. They fled across the open field to the north. On the south side of the road was a terraced village built into the side of a hill, which afforded a spectacular view of our convoy. The Coyote escort car called for medical evacuation and quick reaction force (QRF) assistance. I checked in with RSM Earles. Paddy's eyes were as big as pie plates behind his ballistic glasses. He was travelling in the vehicle behind me and from his perspective; it looked like our diesel truck had been the target. I noticed that he was in full battle mode as I ran back to the crippled Bison. Upon arrival at the Bison I noticed one of our men laid out on the ground behind the ramp where his comrades had been attempting first aid. His wounds were extremely serious and it was obvious he was dead. I later learned that this soldier was Corporal Jason Warren of Montreal. Additionally, the wounds to Corporal Francesco Gomez, the Bison driver, were fatal. He had been killed instantly in the explosion. There were about four of us who worked on the priority one casualties in the Bison. Captain Tony Ross, a PPCLI officer from our S4 (Logistics) cell, had been crew commanding the stricken Bison and he was throwing up from a head trauma. I held his hand and chatted to him. The interior of the Bison was a nightmare blend of dark blood, vomit, Red Bull cans, and empty oatmeal cookie wrappers — a bizarre juxtaposition of the mundane and the real. The QRF medic showed up from the PRT site some 35 minutes later — Petty Officer Mike Cuell. Mike had served with me in Bosnia in 2000 and we knew each other well. Mike Cuell is what I would call an elegant man who, like all our combat medics, deals with the nastiest end of war. I have never known him to either raise his voice or utter a profanity. I helped myself to some on his behalf.

"Holy shit, PO, am I glad to see your ugly mug!" Having the QRF with us was more uplifting than words could convey.

"Sir. Hi. What do you got?" His pupils were screwed tight, and I could see the focused triage going through his mind. Military medics are an absolute marvel. We can never pay them enough, not ever. As a QRF medic in Kandahar City, Mike Cuell had been through this scene many times. In a few moments he had noted our dead and had dialled into the fact that Captain Ross and his head trauma was job number one for medevac.

"Let me in, sir."

I let go of Tony's hand and gladly traded places with Mike in the Bison. There was plenty to do outside. Most of the troops were standing in defensive positions around our stricken convoy, creating a security cordon. Those who weren't engaged in security were needed to recover people and equipment so we could get moving as soon as possible.

"Hey, sir, do you smoke?" a young Canadian soldier I didn't recognize asked me.

"I don't smoke, but I would love a cigarette right now."

The soldier passed me a cigarette and a lighter. I had no idea who he was, but the shared act of normalcy in the middle of chaos stuck with me long after.

We extracted the living casualties to the UH-60 Blackhawk medevac helicopter and put our deceased into the QRF Bison. I always thought that baling hay was the most physically punishing work a human being could undertake. Not anymore. There is a good reason that the army keeps medical evacuation as part of its physical fitness testing. By the time we loaded our second casualty onto the UH-60, my legs were like rubber and I was winded. The Blackhawk air crew were purpose-driven and efficient. They took our high-priority casualties and whistled away off that highway as quick as a dream. The aviation task force consists of some very brave Americans. Task Force Knight Hawk, they called themselves. They were fabulous.

Crowder and I gathered a number of Canadian rifles and pistols off the road and threw them into our truck. It was strange to gather a big bundle of rifles, some damaged and warped by the blast and others not. The service rifle is so tightly controlled and accounted back home and here we were scraping them up off the ground like a vagrant might snatch at $1,000 bills. We grabbed as many as we could recognize. Ancient truths being relearned. Damaged or not there was no way in hell that we were leaving Canadian arms behind on that road. The latter thought was just going through my head when I felt the second enemy detonation. I felt the blast on my face before my ears were treated to it. Our cavalry had been hit. As the QRF was leaving the cordon, a second suicide attack occurred. My heart sank. *Oh, shit. We're not going to get out of here.*

The second attack hadn't penetrated our cordon, waiting instead for the QRF to exit the cordon with our dead. The suicide bomber in this case was wearing a vest full of metal, ball bearings, et cetera over the explosive. There were many Afghan casualties in the second explosion, but no Canadian ones. Only one Mercedes G-Wagon belonging to the great Lieutenant Catton, the QRF commander, had been damaged. Catton had become known affectionately throughout the Task Force as Forrest Gump. He had endured the unpleasant experience of having a rocket-propelled grenade puncture the Mercedes G-Wagon he had been riding in on a convoy in early February. The grenade entered the armoured door and passed under the passenger seat, making its exit on the other side. Catton had remarkably escaped with only minor wounds to his buttocks, which spawned the Hollywood nickname.

By this time my head was swimming with clipped conversations with soldiers, with Crowder, with Paddy. My sense for the passage of time was warped, but I remember clearly the sense that we were losing our daylight. I was certain that the Taliban weren't done with us. We needed to get moving before darkness fell completely. "Rage, rage against the dying of the light" — a fragment of Dylan Thomas popped into my head as I went forward to the second blast area. I noticed a blue car streaking up into the terraced village after the second attack, and there was no doubt in my mind that they were involved in the attack but they were moving too quickly in an area replete with civilians so we did not engage them. I felt completely impotent and ineffective in letting them go. The enemy was playing with us, kicking our asses. In terms of our own situation, all the heavy wreckers were now full of vehicle casualties from the past day of convoy activity. If we could not tow Lieutenant Catton's G-Wagon with a light vehicle, I was contemplating destroying it in place. An Afghan approached me and asked for help with their wounded. I directed him to the Afghan National Police site leader. There were by now a number of civilian ambulances on the scene and our hands were full with our own problems.

It turned out that Catton's G-Wagon was ambulatory. I muttered a prayer of thanks as we dropped it onto a Bison A-Frame. At that moment, two Apache gunships materialized above us, having been sent by Multinational Brigade HQ to assist with our deliverance. The mean-looking machines appeared overhead like two angels of the Lord. They stayed over us while we slowly got underway and made our way through the liquid black streets of Kandahar to our PRT camp. Even before we set a foot inside the PRT, the word was already out in the local media that the stricken Canadian convoy had fired into the crowd and caused a large number of civilian casualties. It was a fabrication and I set the record straight immediately, calling Colonel Tom Putt, General Fraser's deputy, back at the Canadian headquarters on KAF.

"Have you heard what's on the wire?" I blurted.

"I have." He was as balanced and unexcitable as a seasoned Confederate warhorse. Good old Colonel Putt.

"I give you my word, Tom. We didn't fire on those civilians. It's simply not true."

"I know, John, I know. Don't fuss it. It's all good now. Are you coming back in tonight?"

Tom had replied as casually as if he were confirming my Tim Hortons sandwich order. Something in his laidback tone and his unconditional acceptance of my observations settled me, made me feel better.

"No, sir. No way. We'll hunker down here with Simon for tonight. The guys are bushed."

By this time the soldiers had been up for nearly 24 straight hours and they had dealt with enough. It was an easy decision if not an inspired one. The battle-precious supplies, our raison d'être, were in 1 PPCLI's hands. Moreover, the battle group was back on KAF after nearly a month of combat and we could afford a delay for ourselves.

"It's the right call, old man," Tom said. "I'll see you tomorrow. All is good."

I heard the click of the receiver put down back at KAF. I did indeed feel like an old man.

The action of 22 July wasn't dissimilar to many other days in the complex operating environment that was Kandahar. Like so many incidents on our tour, the day was filled with shocking vignettes. It had been heart-wrenching to watch Afghan adults wrap up their children in blankets and scarves — the all-too-familiar practice of harvesting their dead.

Faces approaching me, military and civilian alike asking for help, seeking direction. The relentless coming and going of people and objects into my tunnel vision. What the hell was all of that? Where does the razor-sharp clarity, stretched over such a long number of hours, come from? Adrenaline? A second hand on my Seiko that took forever to advance, a civilian pickup truck with bodies piled in its box, blood streaming down the tailgate and over the bumper, the unmistakable smells that your senses try not to acknowledge, the remains of the first suicide bomber being taken away in a Glad garbage bag. I felt responsible for the violence and victimized at the same time. I parked my emotions and reflection in a far recess in my mind. In the centre of all these razor-sharp vignettes, I neither lost nor obtained complete control. My longest moment of combat was an unflattering series of gropes and grabs at what my mind told me were good solutions. Together we pushed, however clumsily, to achieve what had to be done.

Kandy, an Afghan interpreter who worked in my NSE contracting office on KAF with Major Pete Bayne, had a cousin killed at the double IED attack on 22 July. Kandy had heard the whispers about Canadian soldiers firing into the crowd, allegedly killing many innocent Afghan bystanders, Kandy's cousin among them. He approached me about a week later to ask me about the day.

"Sir, I heard a terrible thing about last Saturday," he ventured awkwardly.

"The ambush west of the city?"

"Yes, sir."

"What was it, Kandy?"

"My cousin was killed in the ambush. He was just standing in the area ... I heard that the Canadians opened fire on the crowd."

"That's an awful story. I can tell you, Kandy, that it's also untrue. Canadian soldiers simply don't act that way. I was there. I can assure you that the killing was done by the Taliban, particularly the second attacker."

"Yes, sir." His tone was like that of a child who had just been chastised.

"Kandy?"

"Sir?"

"I'm so sorry about the loss of your cousin. It was a terrible way to die."

OPERATION MOUNTAIN THRUST

I was afraid many times in Kandahar in 2006. I can honestly tell you that the worst of my nightmares and the ugliest of my demons have not been of Taliban manufacture, they have instead been anchored in the fear of my tiny logistic unit running out of critical *matériel* or human capital. This came home to roost in July when the seams of the unit could be heard to pop on occasion and when the ammunition shortage — my greatest mistake — reared its ugly head. Like one of those treadmills in the gym, with its black conveyor belt moving faster and faster, the pace of life in the logistics battalion accelerated. The workload of the NSE (what we refer to in military jargon as our operational tempo) continued to pick up throughout the entire seven month tour, hitting a fever pitch in July. We expected things to remain hectic throughout the traditional Taliban campaign season that seems to fire up in April and peter out in August. There were two noticeable spikes in tempo. The first was April as we conducted operations and also began building FOB Martello in northern Kandahar. FOB Martello was a major combat engineer effort but it was also a burden for an underweight logistic unit. Changing our concept of operations to decentralized FOBs instead of pooled support on KAF was hard on the logistics soldiers, kind of like sharpening a lawnmower blade while the mower was busy cutting grass. The pace also kicked up an octave in the month of June 2006 when Operation Mountain Thrust began. Most dramatically, the wheels of the running machine nearly came off in July.

Operation Mountain Thrust had been the focus of our planning and preparations for almost all of May. Now it was upon us, a division sized operation. This operation in RC South was the biggest Coalition offensive against the Taliban since they had fallen in 2002. The intent was to dampen the recent spread of insurgent violence in southern Afghanistan. Operation Mountain Thrust involved some 11,000 U.S., British and Canadian troops. Instead of laying back and reacting to insurgents, Mountain Thrust sought to take the offensive and move toward squashing the Taliban hotspots. The operation targeted four of Afghanistan's 34 provinces, the four in which Taliban forces were massed: Helmand, Kandahar, Uruzgan, and Zabul. The idea was to squeeze out the insurgents from these areas, a sort of military chemotherapy in order to set conditions for stability. Once the security problem was curtailed, humanitarian aid and Afghan government institutions could go into these areas and develop a foothold.

The logistics plan for Mountain Thrust called for the NSE to support operations throughout Kandahar Province, focusing primarily in the area of Panjwayi, Zhari, and Maywand. Initial plans saw a concerted effort in Kandahar Province that would have been relatively easy to support, given how busy we had been in May. We had been greatly stretched to in April and May supporting 1 PPCLI in Helmand while building the new Canadian FOB in northern Kandahar Province. Building up FOB Martello had been hard but now that we had it as a secure platform, we had a base that was perfectly suited to sustaining us through Operation Mountain Thrust. I was home on leave in Canada so Scott McKenzie represented the NSE at the divisional logistics war game presided over by General Benjamin Freakley, the American commander of CJTF 76 headquarters. At these war games, the myriad plans of all elements of the forthcoming operation are discussed and reviewed and sometimes altered based on how the war game plays out. Major Paul MacDonald, the J4 operations at inside General Fraser's Multinational Brigade told me that our plan and concept had been extremely well received by General Freakley. It seemed to me that the investment in FOB Martello was about to pay dividends. FOB Martello would be a stable and convenient platform from which we could sustain the Canadian portion of Operation Mountain Thrust, a solid rock in the support plan away from the central hub of KAF. For once we would have a relatively easy support job. I was wrong. Operation Mountain Thrust was about to stretch Canadian logistics lines farther than they had ever been stretched in combat.

Despite the best-laid plans and preparations most of the Canadian operations happened a long way from the spanking new FOB Martello. No matter how much planning and preparation you put into your activities, the enemy always gets to vote on how things will in fact unfold — not the deciding vote, but a vote nonetheless. The Canadian battle plans quickly expanded during the operation when Canadian troops were required in Helmand Province, which was the United Kingdom's responsibility. Of course, we had no logistics basing in Helmand. Ammunition, fuel, and food would have to be carried. The investment in FOB Martello that had tied up so much logistic effort in April and May brought us little relief in supporting Mountain Thrust.

By this point in the tour we had begun to discover the age-old truths about war and relearned many things our fathers and grandfathers knew about warfare. Even the little things had the power to shock. One small but telling issue came up in late June. With our long supply chain and our desperation to keep certain fast-moving supplies in stock, we had been in the habit of putting the clothing and some of the personal equipment of our wounded soldiers back in the warehouse for reissue. This was a big no-no. When soldiers would come in for a new pair of combat pants and see the name of their comrade on the inside label it understandably upset them. You cannot give another soldier the equipment of a dead or wounded comrade without effecting morale. We strove to create the illusion for the infantry that we had an endless supply of stores and equipment but this was clearly a technique that had to stop. We elected to quarantine this sort of *matériel* for use on the next rotation by a group of soldiers who wouldn't have as close a personal connection to the soldiers wounded on our tour. It was a small thing, but it stood out, as it showed how we were relearning some of the ways of war.

On 23 June, Heather Morrison burst into my office and announced that there was a large fire in the Maintenance Platoon's area. Master Corporal Crowder and I grabbed our truck and headed up to the compound taking note of the large dark column of smoke in the distance. The fire had been caused by the accidental discharge of smoke canister from a Bison, which had not been properly unloaded. There were no injuries, however the property damage was extensive and included the LAV fighting vehicle repair shop and all the contents. There was also serious damage to two Bison armoured vehicles that would necessitate their repatriation to Canada for level 3 repairs and overhaul. I looked at the charred Bisons, melted rifle stocks, and blackened tools and test equipment and felt physically ill. The overall impact was a significant clean-up effort by Maintenance Platoon and the temporary loss of workspace and tooling. The really scary outcome was that we lost capacity in LAV III repair at a critical point in the operation. At a time when we would have profited greatly from any increase in capacity, we lost one fifth of our ability to fix the LAVs. The Maintenance Platoon worked around the clock to clean up the debris and build a new workshop for fighting vehicles. Their Herculean effort limited the drastic loss in repair capacity to only one week.

The closure of the Gumbad safe house in northern Kandahar Province on 27 June 2006 was a welcome relief to the Canadian task force. The NSE convoys working hand in glove with Kirk Gallinger's Alpha Company had been finding it increasingly difficult to continue to provide support to this area. The closure required two full days of effort from the NSE Transportation Platoon. The gritty truck drivers provided heavy lift vehicles to extract Alpha Company stores and equipment. A lot of Canadian blood had been spilled to maintain the presence there. With Gumbad gone, Alpha Company was able to concentrate its soldiers and *matériel* in FOB Martello to the east, which sat like a jewel in a crown of otherwise rugged lunar terrain.

KANDAHAR OVERDRIVE

The bottom dropped out of things for us during the month of July. Heather Morrison's support plans became more and more rudimentary as they were crafted and briefed. Complicated logistics movements were reduced to pen sketch out of a spiral bound notebook or a rough drawing on a white board in the command post. The long support distances over to Helmand and the time it took to traverse them left no time for staff college niceties. The soldiers of the NSE could feel that the support situation was serious and convoy turnarounds were tight. Sleep deprivation, always a issue on operations, hit a dangerous level. It was a long way to go to get to the infantry. Ian Hope had told me that Task Force Orion had become a killing machine by the middle of this month, and this proficiency caused the tempo to be kicked up for the NSE. It would be the final pivotal month of our operations with the United States under the Enduring Freedom mandate. NATO's ISAF was poised to take the reins for Regional Command South on 31 July 2006 as part of the overall

ISAF transition plan. Bit by bit, western support in Afghanistan was harmonized under NATO and our country had played a historical role in making it possible. NATO's arrival also converged with a concentration of Taliban fighters in the collection of hamlets known as Pashmul in the Panjwayi District some 25 kilometres from Kandahar. Major Grimshaw's Bravo Company had been in contact with this gathering storm for most of the tour and before we could hand over the reins, another battle was going to be fought in Pashmul.

The fighting in Helmand was part of the larger CJTF 76 Operation Mountain Thrust. Task Force Orion took part in Operation Heward, which was to be the last stanza of the larger divisional operation. We had logistic crews out with the battle group to sustain them in the Sangin District. A number of Tactical Assembly Areas (TAAs) were created along Highway 1 to effect sustainment into Helmand. TAAs are like mini FOBs, tiny defended nodes from which logistics support could be drawn far from the big base at KAF. Since the distances at which 1 PPCLI were operating exceeded 300 kilometres we needed an additional tool to provide routine replenishment. The TAAs were our main means for effecting this, serving as mini Canadian Tire kiosks, defended staging areas for the projection of combat service support. Besides these TAAs, the NSE also provided echelon detachments to accompany the combat teams as they went north along the Helmand River Valley.

Operation Heward ended 17 July 2006, along with the completion of the large offensive that was Mountain Thrust. The battle group was to return to KAF the following day for some refurbishment and much needed rest. The NSE was looking forward to the end of the operation. The comfortable, centralized support concept for Operation Mountain Thrust had flown out the window. It had been a long, hard road keeping Task Force Orion sustained. It was about to get much worse.

In the wee hours of 18 July, Ian Hope was woken from a deep sleep beside his tactical command post. Radio orders were coming in from Brigadier-General Fraser back at KAF. Instead of coming home, Hope received radio orders to turn about 180 degrees and retake two district centres that had fallen to the Taliban in the southern Helmand River Valley, Nawa and Garmisher. Had these two district centres not been recovered

President Karzai's government would have been seriously discredited. The situation simply could not stand. Hope used his Alpha and Charlie Companies to restore order to the two centres. There were no written operation orders and accompanying administrative instructions for our support plan. There was no time. The action had to be taken and there was no time for staff college orders and preparations. It is fascinating to hear Major Kirk Gallinger, the officer commanding Alpha Company, talk about his combat team attack in Garmisher. At one point the attack became so chaotic that he actually hauled everyone back and launched again.

I am still not completely certain how we kept the task force in gear during this period. Looking back on it now, it seems impossible. The Canadian lines of supply during this period stretched at times as much as 350 kilometres (one way) from KAF. This length of resupply line had never been entertained in my or anyone else's approach to building the NSE. It is an understatement to say that this discreet mission kept the unit extremely busy. The significance of the length and duration of these lines of operations cannot be overstated. It is akin to supporting a large trucking company of some 300 vehicles in Toronto from Kingston, except that when delivering fuel, food, and supplies in Afghanistan, you can only travel back roads. For 1 PPCLI, there were no service stations, no places to stop along the Helmand River Valley for ammunition, water, or diesel. Replenishment all had to be dragged along by the NSE from KAF hundreds of dangerous kilometres away and through the volatile Zhari District, which sits just north of Panjwayi. This is a line of communication that most field commanders would never have accepted in the past. The accomplishment is all the more significant when the fluid nature of the non-contiguous battlefield is considered. Field Marshal Montgomery, the famous commander of 21st Army Group in northwest Europe, wouldn't tolerate lines of communication for his army group that exceeded 150 kilometres. In Montgomery's context, the battlefield was more predictable and significantly safer away from the thunder of the front line. Many of these 150 kilometres that had to be covered by his Second World War logisticians would fall into the communication zone away from the forward edge of combat. In Kandahar and Helmand, every kilometre of every convoy harboured the potential to become a combat operation. Every time our soldiers mount their vehicles they would brace for the possibility of a blast. Never in the history of Canadian arms has such a small logistics team supported such a robust combat force over these distances and duration.

> Jesus, I am off to call Mrs. Earles. I will never tell her about what almost happened to us. I can't. It would kill her.
>
> — Chief Warrant Officer Pat Earles[81]

On 22 July 2006, nearly a week over schedule, Task Force Orion finally set out to come back from Helmand. The NSE mounted a large commodity convoy to set up a commodity point to furnish the battle group return from Helmand. This activity signified the end of Canadian operations in Helmand, and the NSE column returned to Kandahar as part of the larger battle group move. Regrettably, the logistics convoy was attacked on the western edge of Kandahar in a double suicide bomber attack (described earlier in this chapter) that saw the column halted for nearly two hours before extraction was possible.

Ninety-five percent of the fighting my soldiers did was with themselves, in the kingdom of the mind. It takes mental toughness to mount your vehicle and head out on convoy when every car that passes looks like a bomb. Mental toughness is the backbone of success in the new sort of battlefields our soldiers find themselves on. The moral strength, even of a robust unit, can reach a tipping point. My God, but we came close to finding ours.

We achieved much in seven months of intense operations. None of those months was more fraught with quiet desperation than those 30-odd days from 7 July to 5 August. We had no business doing what we did over such crushing distances and perilous enemy-infested terrain. The about turn of the Canadian battle group on 17 July to liberate the district centres of Nawa and Garmisher, by just about anyone's concept of combat service support, should have snapped our logistics linkage with Ian Hope. But our soldiers, the soldiers of the columns, would not let it break. They maintained a supply line over 300 kilometres long for nearly three weeks. The NSE was too small for its tasks even when events were confined to Kandahar Province. That month of overdrive, when we helped our British neighbours in Helmand Province, there was something very Vimy Ridge about what Task Force Orion had done. What we had done.

13

Losing Ray

Ishould never have pulled back the ballistic blanket. Major Scott McKenzie had quickly discerned that Master Corporal Raymond Arndt, lying in a crumpled heap on the highway, was dead. McKenzie had put the makeshift shroud over Arndt before helping with the casualties in the convoy who were still fighting to live. Ray was one of our most popular convoy escort soldiers, a tough infantryman from Alberta's Loyal Edmonton Regiment. He was dead, but I dearly wanted to tell him goodbye. The only feature immediately recognizable under the blanket was his hand slightly raised above his broken body, making a last noble gesture from death's other kingdom to the living world and the people who loved him. He was a great soldier and a truly inspirational person.

Paddy and I lumbered up the stairs of Task Force Orion on 23 July. I had Tony Ross's ruined 9 mm Browning pistol and about half of the rifles we collected at the scene of yesterday's suicide attack. Two men had been killed and another eight wounded, and between us we had tried to recover all their personal weapons. Paddy had the rest of the rifles clutched tightly in those determined Newfoundlander mitts of his. Lieutenant-Colonel Hope was in a closed door meeting in his plywood office but Todd Strickland, Hope's excellent deputy, rapped his knuckles on the office door and ushered us inside without a single word.

Our eyes met briefly, and I looked away to the right to the room's only other occupant. The other man was Randy Northrup, Ian's own

RSM. Randy studied the pair of us with his eyes, stopping longest on the heaps of weapons we were toting, then glanced quickly back at Hope.

"We missed you yesterday. Got strung out from you," I started awkwardly.

"We were already home when you were hit," Ian said as Paddy and I set the weapons on the worn Persian carpet that served as the only badge of civility in the battle group commander's office. The rug was a remnant left behind by Burt Ges, Hope's American predecessor. The Canadian column returning from Helmand was over 20 kilometres long, and with our logistics vehicles at the rear it was easy to get brushed farther back with vehicle breakdowns, like being the last child in the human chain we used to call the whip in the schoolyard.

"The pistol is Tony's. We aren't too sure who owns what where the C7s are concerned. They were spread out all over the site."

"What a terrible day," Ian offered, and I recall him saying something about the long war, the long road.

"Ian, there was nothing I could have done for Warren and Gomez. I —"

Hope cut me off. "Of course not." His eyes met mine, and in them I saw firm recognition of the edgeless guilt aflame in my conscience. "Of course not."

In those three clipped words from my trusted colleague I found legions of comfort.

> The boot is supplied in whole and half sizes 3 through 14 in all widths ... In some instances it may be necessary to make a size adjustment in order to obtain an adequate fit due to normal swelling of the feet ...
>
> — Instruction Tag for Type II,
> Canadian Boots, Hot Weather

Just as the U.S. Army has discovered in Iraq, we have learned that you can't get combat arms soldiers to escort logistics columns. There simply aren't enough armoured and infantry soldiers to do it. On our tour, 1 PPCLI was stretched to the limit and the only time we would get a LAV III infantry escort was when the column happened to be going the same way as an available LAV III or Coyote reconnaissance car. Truly, the best way to get infantry to escort your convoys is to grow your own and that is exactly what we did with the Defence and Security Platoon. This organization of 34 soldiers consisted of reserve infantry from Alberta. Ian Hope's organization had brushed them up on their basic infantry tactics and they came over to me for convoy escort training in Wainwright in the fall of 2005. They were smart soldiers, fast learners. Our investment in time, training, and administration in that little platoon paid dividends for the NSE throughout the tour. Most of the young men in the platoon were either University of Calgary or University of Alberta students, including Lieutenant Rob Gliddon, the commander. Christie Blatchford had dubbed Rob the "baby-faced" platoon commander in one of her articles for the *Globe and Mail*. The handle had stuck to the fourth-year University of Alberta engineering student like glue. It was true. Rob was shockingly youthful in appearance, but then again so were the men he led. However, baby-faced Gliddon and his team were no slouches. What the platoon lacked in experience they more than overcame with energy and personality.

I wanted these young militia soldiers to know they had a home and a position of prime importance in the wider battalion. Too often in our recent past, cultural divisions between the reserve and regular force lead to rifts in units. There was a time when many soldiers in the regular force considered our part-time militia soldiers to be of inferior quality. This sentiment has changed dramatically over the past several years to the point where the army now plans to send part-time soldiers on operations in substantial numbers. Despite the changed perception toward the reserve soldier, remnants of prejudice exist and it was important to me that our reservists were not subjected to that. We needed them so badly.

A comprehensive 10-day training plan was executed for my militia infantry platoon. The package was designed to take the platoon from Level 3 live to include convoy orders, reaction to IED and ambush and operating the LUVW gun truck/firing on the move. This package received the full attention of the unit and was validated by the RSM and myself both in Tarnak Farms Range and in the conduct of the platoon's first operational escort task into Kandahar City. The performance of this Alberta-based platoon was exceptional. They had absorbed all the tactical and equipment training requirements put to them. LUVW-based, gun truck escort is a most viable future role for militia infantry and in my opinion should be further explored by the Corps of Infantry.

Falling in love with each other was difficult. Even before Paddy Earles and I landed in Kandahar on 11 February, one of the reserve sergeants had shot one of my warrant officers, a regular force mechanic, in the leg in the airfield tent lines. It was a horrible accident that could easily have ended up with fatalities. The 9 mm round had travelled through a number of tent walls and under soldiers' cots before it found its resting place in the calf of an NSE warrant officer. The senior soldiers of the Maintenance Platoon had their blood up, and for many troops looking in on this terrible accident, the spectres of prejudice and distrust percolated among them. A lot of my senior non-commissioned members wanted the sergeant involved punished and sent home — immediately. "Goddamn reservists!" was heard more than once in the tent lines. Experienced soldiers have a most effective way of communicating advice and wisdom and they were as subtle as a jackhammer in their messaging to me. I did not send the reserve infantry sergeant home. He was punished in accordance with the book but we kept him on in that critical leadership rank. He ended up as a convoy escort leader on nearly 120 convoys and a Canadian veteran and a folk hero in the eyes of his unit in Kandahar. It was the case of an excellent man making an awful mistake, and I thank providence that we were able to discern this and keep the sergeant in Kandahar. We would have been enormously weakened to lose him.

The soldiers of the reserve infantry platoon had their own prejudices and stereotypes to keep them on edge as well. They were angry at battalion headquarters after we arrived in Kandahar. It seemed to them that their equipment was the last to be handed out and they fumed waiting in line for their machine-gun-equipped Mercedes G-Wagons. The truth of the matter was that all Mercedes G-Wagons were going through a refit of their turret rings which were becoming dislodged on Afghanistan's brutal roads. Our gun trucks were no later than anyone else's but deeply ingrained mindsets are slow to be dislodged. To make matters worse from their perspective, once they got their gun trucks, I insisted on the reserve platoon going through an additional 10 days of rigorous training with the new equipment at Tarnak Farms. One of my senior operations officers, the erudite Captain Ken Bloom, designed a fantastic package to give the soldiers a better feel for firing their weapons on the move and working with the heavier, slower logistic wagons. Well, to put them through this training you would have thought I had slapped their faces. These young soldiers wanted to get out on Afghanistan's roads and win the war immediately. It reminded me of the stories of the First World War when Canadian recruits wanted to get to France immediately out of fears that the war would be over by Christmas. We had the time to do it right. The campaign in Afghanistan is going well, but as the Canadian public is learning, it is not a mission that will be achieved in a month or a year. We could afford two weeks for ourselves. Those early days of March were electric with expectation, early attacks by the Taliban and yet there we stood in relative safety at Tarnak going through a series of pretend attacks with the Defence and Security Platoon.

When RSM Paddy Earles and I were happy with their training, we mounted up to be escorted by the platoon on their first real convoy into Kandahar City. This maiden voyage was set for 8 March. The night before the convoy I finished my last letter to my family, which remained tucked inside my barrack box for the duration of the tour. I jotted a few notes in my orders book: "First mission for the Reserve Platoon. They are young, confident and ready ... I am off to Nathan Smith at 1000 hrs. Wish us luck. Martha, Aidan, Morgan, Harriet, and Grace, I love you all! 7 March 2006."

The convoy, excepting a mechanical breakdown on Highway 1, went well and we turned the escort reins for our city convoys over to Gliddon and his fountain of youth. They never disappointed us and they continued to shock me with their accomplishments and ability to acquire new skills and responsibilities. The parents of these men have every right to be proud of their sons. By the end of the tour, most of these men had completed more than 100 convoys in southern Afghanistan. Not all these troops were able to finish the tour owing to injuries, and one of them, Raymond Arndt, was killed, but the soldiers of Defence and Security Platoon who returned home had an honorary godfather for the rest of their lives.

In the early days we used the Defence and Security Platoon to escort east-west convoys between KAF and Kandahar City proper. The majority of escorts for convoys north were provided by the battle group. They were good at it. Over the course of the tour, the militia platoon did so well that they earned themselves more work, picking up additional convoy escort duties on north and south trips as the battle group became busier. By the end of June, they had taken over most of the escort tasks for the CSS task vehicles freeing up Task Force Orion to focus it forces on primarily combat operations. Given the number of resupply runs and the travel time between KAF and FOBs, this was a significant undertaking for a Force Protection Platoon that is seeing them conducting almost a convoy per day.

Until I read Christie Blatchford's book *Fifteen Days*, I never knew the actual sizes of Raymond Arndt's feet. His right foot was a size nine and his left a size six. I knew he had a birth defect and that one foot was, well, slightly smaller than the other. Learning after Raymond's death that the difference was three whole sizes just reminded me of the determination he possessed and the triumph of the human spirit. Ray had wanted to be a soldier so badly that this physical challenge had no hope of holding him back from joining the infantry. Ray was part of the young infantry militia platoon, the Defence and Security Platoon, I had for convoy escort. The RSM and I went down to the platoon lines to express our sense of loss and grief the night Ray died. The fine soldiers of that militia platoon were so young, so full of life and when they met my eyes with their collective grief it stirred me. I was careful with my words to honour the memory of our comrade. I shook each of their hands after my brief chat and there were tears in my eyes when the RSM and I walked away.

Two days after the fifth battle at Pashmul the dust was still settling in the deadly collection of villages that have become synonymous with the Taliban stronghold. We had paid with our best heart's blood to realize that a brigade, not a battalion-sized attack, would be required to suppress the insurgents in that area. On 5 August the ramp ceremony for four Canadians was disquieting. It was the second time on our tour that we sent four fallen home at once. The emotions it conjures up inside you are powerful. These men were tough, four outstanding infantry soldiers —

perfect men, as Hope referred to them. Scott was going out today with a convoy bound for Spin Boldak. It was a sad enough day, but it was about to get worse:

> Only a couple of hours after the ramp ceremony, I was getting ready to head down in a convoy to one of our remote camps to show the place to two guys from the new team that is replacing my unit. It had already been a pretty crappy day ... I was tired, frustrated and annoyed. The convoy departure got delayed with bunch of confusion about loading passengers, and waiting around in the heat wasn't making it any better. Finally we headed off on our way, about an hour late.
> — Major Scott McKenzie, "Afghanistan Updates"

Master Corporal Shawn Crowder was driving in the convoy that morning. He was the first to notice that the G-Wagon, the rear gun truck, was in trouble:

> Approx 22 kilometres south of KAF we passed by three large Jingle trucks that were heading northbound and appeared to be travelling slowly as we drove by. I remember that the vehicles hadn't moved over very far to the side of the road as most vehicles do when we are approaching. I had to move my vehicle over from the centre of the roadway to the right side of the road. The left side of my vehicle was either at the centre line or just over when I passed by the Jingle trucks. After I passed the Jingle trucks, I looked in my left mirror and saw the GSK involved in a collision with one of the Jingle trucks. I saw the GSK when it was almost completely sideways on the road and it started to leave the ground. I immediately told Major McKenzie, my co-driver, to "get on the radio and tell everyone to turn around now! The GSK is rolling." I then immediately slammed on the brakes

and turned around as fast as I could and got back to the accident scene at the best speed possible.

Master Corporal Arndt's platoon provided convoy escort for logistic columns and he himself had escorted some 85 to 90 convoys when this accident caused his untimely death. That was a lot of action on the lava lamp battlefield. Also injured in the accident were Corporal Jared Gagnon, Corporal Ash van Leeuwen, and Private Adam Keen. Private Keen recovered quickly in KAF and returned to duty. As I write, both Corporals Gagnon and van Leeuwen are progressing well at home in Canada. Scott had attended the ramp ceremony for the four dead Canadians from Pashmul and then mounted up for the trip to Spin Boldak. He tells it best:

> It was a small convoy, with three vehicles ahead of me (one of which was a personnel carrier with the passengers we waited for) my vehicle, and then the rear escort vehicle which was a LUVW (armoured jeep) with a gun mount.
>
> We were about 20 minutes out of KAF heading down a decent part of the road, which was heavy with traffic, when my driver shouted that the veh [vehicle] behind us had been in an accident (they had run head on into a local truck hauling cattle that suddenly crossed the middle of the road) and started to turn the vehicle around (we knew we were now last in the convoy and would have to do some local security). I got on the radio and informed the lead vehicle of the accident and told him to stop the convoy. Once we were turned around and I could see the accident site, the guts dropped out of me. The vehicle was on the road resting on its roof and I could see at least three soldiers strewn along the road. I got on the radio again to confirm the accident was very bad, to get the convoy turned around, and get the medic up ASAP. I then ran another 10 metres or so to the next soldier, and although I was there only about

30 seconds after the accident, it was obvious he was dead for the extent of his injuries and the colour of his skin. Thinking we had two dead soldiers on our hands, I ran on to the last soldier ... Then I ran to the vehicle to get on the radio to tell them we had one dead for sure and two serious casualties.

Back in the command post I hung on every word in that was coming in, hoping against hope that the initial report of "vital signs absent" was incorrect. Crowder and McKenzie were in the column. All I could think of was that Scott's wife, Catherine, was expecting their first child back in Edmonton. Shawn Crowder, a man who had grown to be like a little brother to me, was a father and sole breadwinner in a young military family. His wife had just been released by the Canadian Forces. Please, dear God, it cannot be them. In the next nanosecond I felt guilty for the thought. All these troops were my boys; any of them being lost would be a tragedy. Major McKenzie continues in his "Afghanistan Updates":

That done I headed back to the wounded soldiers to start first aid. The two passengers in my vehicle were already working on the first soldier (one of them was advanced trauma first aid qualified) so I headed to the less injured soldier and started working. In seconds the medic was there followed by the passengers from the Bison (infantry soldiers from C Coy of the battle group who I found out later were all pallbearers during the morning's ramp ceremony if you can believe that). I briefed the medic on the situation and knowing the C Coy boys had more first aid trg [training] than me, I turned work over to them and got back on the radio. The latest report being radioed in, I turned to the job of positively identifying the dead soldier (that was actually a difficult task in his condition) and once I had confirmed who it was, I used some Kevlar blankets from our vehicle to cover him up. The rest is pretty much a blur until the casevac choppers showed up. I coordinated security on the site, got the interpreter talking to some local police that showed up, got them to call for more and ran around getting things for the medic. That done, I took up a security spot myself and kept an eye on the guys providing first aid to the soldier with the head wound. Everyone worked incredibly hard, especially given the heat, and although we thought we had lost him several times, we managed to keep him alive long enough for the choppers to arrive.

He and the other soldier were evacuated back to KAF for treatment, and as of right now they are in Germany at the U.S. hospital (the third soldier had a compound leg fracture, a broken ankle, and eight broken ribs). We all anxiously await news of the soldier with the head injury and although he is in bad shape it appears for now he is at least stable. After the choppers left, we started cleaning up the area, picking up all the kit that was strewn about the road and gathering the personal belongings of the hurt soldiers.

While McKenzie was dealing with all of this, I made the decision that I would go out there and assist with the recovery of the convoy. It was a poor decision. In my role, I had no need to go. I was fighting a deep conviction to go after them and as so often happens in my life, I made the emotional decision. These were my boys. I would get them. Paddy grabbed his rifle, and away we went with the 1 PPCLI quick reaction force.

Soon after a recovery team came for the vehicle, along with additional security, and ambulance to pick up the dead soldier, and a padre for last rites. Once all was cleaned up we all turned around and headed back to KAF. The whole thing lasted about three hours.

What is the worst about this whole incident is these soldiers were from my unit and the dead soldier was a soldier I had spent a lot of time with during convoys. He was an excellent, professional soldier with a great sense of humour who was really well liked throughout the unit. Although losing any CA soldier is terrible, I had always hoped we would not lose one of our own. I certainly never wanted to be there when it happened, but there I was. This was certainly the worst experience of my tour, and one I will not forget.

— Major Scott McKenzie, "Afghanistan Updates"

I couldn't get my thoughts to focus as we made our way slowly back to KAF in convoy. I was fixated on watching an expensive Camelback water canteen as it bounced and twisted at the rear of the crumpled G-Wagon. The equipment had somehow become lodged under the frame of the vehicle's back door and it scraped along Highway 4. The image was almost as unsettling as looking at its former owner.

I wrote a letter of condolence to Ray's widow, Darcy Arndt, back in Edmonton. I spent a full day getting my thoughts framed, imagining my own wife reading a similar document. I printed it off and showed it to my adjutant, Captain Christine Bruce, for a discreet second opinion.

"Sir, I've finished the letter. I think it's very good. Here's a pen and good paper for you to write the last draft."

"Pen? Paper?" I mused aloud.

"Sir, you have to do this letter in handwriting."

"Of course." Christine was totally right. The damn adjutant turns up being right more often that not. Thank heavens for smart captains.

The day after Raymond Arndt was killed I returned to the KAF Role 3 Hospital to say goodbye to Ash Van Leeuwen. He was being evacuated to Lahnstuhl, Germany. He was upset and kept apologizing to Paddy and me.

"I'm so sorry, sir. I'm sorry I let you down." His face was wet with tears.

It was utter nonsense. He had done a fantastic job, and I was humbled by the fact that he wanted, after all the kilometres of dangerous convoys, after the fatal results of yesterday's Spin Boldak convoy, what Ash has called, "My Last Afghan Sunrise," he wanted to stay on. Across from Van Leeuwen, Corporal Jared Gagnon lay on his bed unconscious, broken, and yet breathing remarkably evenly. All I could think was that he couldn't have had much time left. He was really, like so many of Rob Gliddon's platoon, not much more than a kid. Sergeant-Major Miles of the RCR had told me how a quart of blood had poured out of Jared's helmet when he recovered it and his blunt soldier's assessment of Jared's wounds left little doubt in my mind that Corporal Gagnon would be lucky to survive a medical evacuation to Germany. Miles, a member of the new NSE that was going to replace us, had been on the first convoy of his tour when the accident occurred. I stayed with Jared Gagnon a long time that night. I prayed over his youthful frame harder than I have prayed for anything in my life.

> I look up to the mountains, from where shall my help
>   come?
> For the men and women of these lumbering logistics
>   columns it has come from
> The likes of MCpl Raymond Arndt
> MCpl Arndt is the sort of soldier I ask for in my prayers
> A tough resilient leader who remained patient and vigi-
>   lant as our
> Convoys lumbered into delay after delay — perpetual
>   setbacks in Afghanistan's crushing heat
> All of these trials were always met with a grin and a nod
> Toughness and eternal patience for an echelon that
>   could not make it without
> The likes of him
> He was our protector and he will always be our brother
> Go gently, dear brother, go gently
> You will never be forgotten.
>   — NSE Tribute to Master Corporal Raymond Arndt
>   at his Ramp Ceremony[82]

THE WISDOM OF THE RAIN

It is not your fault.

I noticed among all of my leaders that they tended to blame themselves when their soldiers got hurt. I was just as bad as my subordinates in this arena and right up to the end of the tour. It took me the entire seven months and most of the next year in Canada to realize that these wounds of war, the human toll on your unit, are not your fault. This is far easier to write and say than it is to practice. You must ensure that the dead are removed with the utmost respect and that the wounded are treated and are consistently well provided for until they return to duty or leave Afghanistan. If you have performed competently and fully discharged these duties you must move on. We, the living, need you. We need you fully invested in the next operation. Recognizing this emotion in myself and talking about the matter with my own senior non-commissioned members and officers gave our leadership a certain Civil War earthiness. This hands-on, grounded feel was exactly what I wanted in my command climate and I think it served us well. The soldiers needed to know that I knew them well. Formality and officious handling had no purchase in the NSE. All 300 of us were in this fight together both inside and outside the wire.

I was criticized during my exit from Afghanistan for taking things too hard when my men were hurt or killed. It is true that you cannot lose it in front of your soldiers. I worked hard to ensure that I never shed tears around any of them and I know I slipped a bit in the aftermath of Ray's death. However, I absolutely believe that the leader has the first duty to remain human under these most inhumane of circumstances. You can, in fact I believe you must, show emotion without losing control or respect. The soldiers will be disturbed if you behave otherwise.

When you lose soldiers, a little piece of you dies along with him or her. That's certainly how I felt overseas. It is how I still feel. Corporal Gomez and Corporal Warren were lost in my convoy right in front of me on 22 July 2006. They were killed instantly and their ramp ceremony left me rocked by emotions I could never have anticipated. I think about 22 July every day, and even though my dreams of Kandahar have ramped down to occasional instead of nightly, I find my thoughts on that same patch of Highway 1, 22 July 2006, every single day. I watched Jason Warren's parents on television on Remembrance Day 2007. They had taken the incredible step of going over to Kandahar themselves to be near where their son had fallen.

It is not your fault.

14

Home on Leave

Mohammed Arif was my friend. He was one of my civilian leaders who spoke an impressive level of English. He was an intelligent man who supervised a team of half a dozen young Afghan men who scrubbed out the battalion headquarters, removed waste, and attended to the manifold sundry chores required by the unit. Mohammed Arif had studied at the University of Kabul in better times. He was once a public school math teacher, and his face lightened up when I told him how weak I was at math. I asked him why he didn't teach anymore. There was a great need for teachers again in Kandahar. He made a sweeping motion with his arms to tell me how big his family was — six children. Working for us was an easy decision. The pay of a math teacher in Kandahar didn't come close to what he made with us on KAF.

"Mohammed Arif, do people here hate us?" I asked after reading a note from my daughter.

He grinned, unsure where this was going. "Excuse me, sir?"

"Would they rather we just go home? Personally, I'm here as long as you need me. I believe in your country's future. But I must tell you, my friend, I have four children of my own back in Canada, and if this isn't working out for Afghanistan, if having Canadian soldiers here is just too repulsive to your countrymen, I would be only too glad to go home. Please tell me the truth, not what you think I'd like to hear."

He stared at me, thinking about his answer. Then his grin evaporated.

"I have to know as a father and a husband. I have to know."

"No, sir. We want things to change and get better. It is much better now with America and NATO. You must stay. Others will come around. They are afraid now, but they will come around."

"How can we get your folks to take the hand that's offered? How do we convince your people that our offer is genuine? Our intent here is genuine. You do believe me, Mohammed Arif?"

"I believe you, sir."

There was still hope among the citizens of this country, and that was enough for me.

I began the long trip home on leave on 4 May 2006 with a Hercules hop from KAF to Mirage. The pressures of late June and July hadn't begun to put the NSE into a full sprint. It was strange coming out of theatre and out of uniform, leaving my weapons in Camp Mirage, the brilliant Canadian staging base at an undisclosed site on the Arabian Peninsula. Camp Mirage is home to the mighty fleet of aging C-130 Hercules aircraft that serve as heroic workhorses for the Canadian Forces in Afghanistan. For Canadian troops, the Hercules is your only ticket into Afghanistan and this impressive fleet of planes runs on a tighter schedule than the Swiss Railways in Zurich. I remember being amused to learn that the soldiers and aircrew of Camp Mirage referred to the trip into Afghanistan as "going north." Going north became the catch phrase around Camp Mirage for heading back into the war zone. Mirage is a much-needed transfer point for our soldiers. It is a safe zone where you begin to grasp that you truly can live again; you will be getting your full life back. It is a potent realization, numbing in its effect. Sitting in the shade of a palm tree and looking at the lonely and level spread of the desert was abundant entertainment for me for many hours. Camp Mirage approximates my own vague notion of heaven, a place where you run into comrades and friends you knew in an earlier, different time in a relaxed new way. I relished the delight of walking around the camp unarmed and unfettered by responsibility.

As I dropped my gear at the camp mess hall the night of 4 May, feeling light and shiny in civilian clothing I learned that Ian Hope was also in camp. He was coming back into theatre from an abbreviated leave in Costa Rica. Seeing Hope in this alternate universe was odd but fantastic. He cracked out some fine Cuban cigars and we sat smoking and sipping Cokes in the waning heat of the Arabian twilight. I brought him up to speed on the latest operations from Kandahar where his deputy commanding officer, Major Todd Strickland, was doing a spanking good job, having recently commanded a fair portion of the battle group in a combat operation. Todd Strickland, the picture of balance and tolerance, had handled the action with talent and poise. After discussing the latest inside the Canadian Task Force we resumed our neverending debate over U.S. Civil War generalship. The discussion had started in the long waits during the two Afghanistan reconnaissance trips in the fall of 2005. Hope is well read and halfway through his doctorate at Queen's University, and is of the opinion that the blunt attributes of Ulysses S. Grant, the commander of the Union forces, is the top of the heap. For me, however, there can be no equal to the moral genius and talent of General Robert E. Lee. His lasting effect transcended even his battlefield acumen. General Lee carried the hope of his young nation in the palm of his hand in every battle and fought ferociously, unflustered by the gravity of potential tactical failure. General Grant may have fought well for his country, but in the case of Robert E. Lee, he became his country, for in the end, his legacy was all that was left to the south. Ian, of course, feels this is all bullshit.

We ended up sharing one of the Camp Mirage double rooms and getting to bed late. He was returning "going north" the next day and I was going home to my family in Ontario. Angels vetting our dreams that night would have been struck by the contrasts between us. One man was unwinding and learning to walk lightly again among free men while the other was steeling both mind and body for the return to the fight. When I woke up the next morning and began organizing my things for the Canada flight, Hope had already been gone for three hours. I would not have the chance to speak to my friend again until late June when our shared tactical situation was extremely serious. By that time our command posts would be over 300 kilometres apart but pulling hard together in the same direction.

Of course, school was in full swing back in Canada. I took a great deal of delight in marshalling my four kids and putting them on the bus. It was so good to give my wife, Martha a bit of a break. She was visibly tired and worn down by the mission and keeping a semblance of normalcy alive at home. The simple chores of confirming homework assignments and making school lunches seemed to be the perfect tonic to adjusting to peace at home. I was far from comfortable during my holiday. Coming out of theatre, a soldier finds himself trapped between two very different worlds. You cannot get away from a war you are emotionally involved in. I had been out of Canada since 8 February when I left Edmonton. Until my leave, I had not been on the receiving end of the comprehensive media coverage Kandahar was getting in the living rooms of our nation. At every mention of the word on the nightly news my heart rate would pick up. I would check our email at home for any messages from Scott McKenzie in Afghanistan. It absolutely blew my mind that I could send and receive unclassified messages in our 1840 stone farmhouse in Ontario to a high tech combat logistic unit on the other side of the planet. As sick as it sounds, receiving the odd note from my deputy in Afghanistan helped me relax while at home.

The morning of 18 May 2006 the war reached up and slapped my face. I took the kids down the lane and while we waited for the school bus to arrive I glanced down at *The Toronto Star*, all folded and wrapped waiting for me to peruse over coffee, once the bus pulled away. There on the front page of the paper was the warm face of Captain Nichola Goddard looking up at me. It was her "just in case" media release photo taken beside her LAV III. All soldiers in Task Force Afghanistan had to have one. Your final photo or death photo as they grimly came to be known was a picture of you in your full protective gear with your best smile underneath the CF beret that is reserved for only official occasions in Kandahar. The photos were electronically stored and stood ready for release when someone was killed. The death photo was the final face we would put to the world; a last long look back at our fellow Canadians. I remember thinking that Nichola Goddard, Charlie Company's forward observation officer, could not be dead. Nichola was Major Bill Fletcher's dedicated artillery officer, an officer about whom Fletcher had once commented, "I never go anywhere without her." Surely not Nichola who had taught my NSE officers and NCOs how to call down artillery fires during our workup training in Alberta and who had recently attended a modest NSE barbecue for the battle group on KAF. It is a shocking experience losing someone so young and vibrant in a burst of violence. You find yourself replaying the fragments of final moments you shared with them for no particular, sound reason. I remember she had such a vibrant personality and a warm availability. She had expressed some concern over two of the new artillery guns, the M777s, that were being fixed in the NSE workshop the night our unit hosted the battle group officers at a barbecue. The government had purchased six of these new guns specifically for our mission. We had guns Number 1, 2, 3, and 4 in Kandahar, while numbers 5 and 6 were being used at home to train the next rotation gun crews. They were so new that President George W. Bush apparently had to sign an official release document in order for Canada to get them and field them in Afghanistan ahead of the U.S. Marine Corps. The M777 is a revolutionary piece of field artillery that takes advantage of titanium to decrease the weight of what would normally be a very heavy field gun. It has an incredible range and an even more impressive pinpoint accuracy. Its freshness and unusual design, however, meant that many of its parts had to come from industry in the United States and this exclusive supply sourcing made me perpetually edgy. Nichola, the consummate young professional, was concerned. I recalled at that moment reassuring her that the weapons technicians had already cased the problem and our genius Electrical Technical Sergeant-Major, Earle Eastman, had already ordered the required parts. The parts would be in our hands from North America by Monday. In short, her guns would be back in action soon. It was the last time I ever spoke to this wonderful young officer. She had only another two weeks to live. Nichola was killed leading from the front in the vicinity of Pashmul, 20-odd kilometres west of Kandahar. The battle occurred inside the same 1,000 metre square that would see the bulk of 1 PPCLI's fights during our tour. While I was home on leave I received cards and phone calls and best wishes from different Second World War veterans who lived in my community, and I cannot help wondering if this is a common emotional experience of

Canada's earlier wars: an experience that has lain dormant in Canada since the Korean War. Every time I drive past my old alma mater, the Royal Military College, I think of Nichola Goddard relaxing with a soft drink at the NSE barbecue. I was not a good RMC cadet in my own time there: I played lots of rugby, studied little, and longed for the day I would be able to leave. As an ex-cadet, I have never found my groove in what can be a sea of cliques among alumni. Seeing Captain Goddard's shiny new name plate at the base of the old RMC Memorial Arch, I have at last found a deep fondness for RMC. As an educational institution it has its highs and lows that are not for all tastes. However, it is the institution that produces such sterling officers as Major Bill Fletcher and Captain Nichola Goddard. The world can use as many Nichola Goddards as RMC can turn out.

> To Dady. We miss you a lot. When will you come home?
> Say when you will come home. Be saf on your mishin.
> Plese be careful.
>
> Senserely,
> Harriet [Conrad]

When you made a phone call to Canada from KAF, you were immersed immediately in the mental anguish of the mission. No matter how deeply you drilled yourself down into the thinly walled phone cubicles both for personal privacy and consideration of other callers, the comments still assailed you, alarmed you, and moved you with an honesty and power that William Butler Yeats would have envied. The human intensity and sense of a shared weight hung heavy in the air of the phone trailer.

"Mommy can't come home for your birthday sweetie, but I'll be home for Halloween."

"I'm all right," claimed another disembodied voice. "The explosion was three vehicles ahead of me." The faceless voice deftly turned the conversation off Afghanistan with a quick inquiry. "By the way, are you still having trouble with the starter in the Chev?"

The weekly phone call was a difficult experience. I dreaded them because they eroded my moral strength. I dearly wanted to hear my children's voices, but at the same time I had very little I wanted to share with them from Kandahar. I merely wanted to sit there and listen. Martha had sent me a Starbucks travel mug for Easter with photographs of all of our children on it, but I never once took it on convoy. I didn't want them that close to the war. Talking with them on the phone, I felt I had to walk a fine line to maintain a facade of normalcy in their lives back home. But like the coffee mug that stayed in my office on KAF, I didn't want them to come too close to the world I lived in. I recall hearing my oldest son's long-winded explanation about a school project and his latest horse-riding lesson. Listening to his innocent, boyish enthusiasm, so full of energy and love of life, caused tears to well up in my eyes. I missed him dearly and I missed seeing the world as he did.

"What have you been doing, Dad?" he asked me once.

"Nothing too much. I saw a camel out in Helmand this week."

"What's Helmand?"

"Helmand's the province next door to Kandahar, kind of like Manitoba is to Ontario but smaller."

The friggin' Taliban did their best to kill us on the way home.

"Oh, can you get me one of those camel whips that you got for Grandpa?"

"You bet. Hey, Aidan."

"Yeah, Dad?"

"Keep up the good work at school, okay?"

"I will. Love you, Dad."

Oh, Christ I love you, too, but I just can't talk right now. Someday I'll tell you everything. I'll lay it all out for you, but not now.

"Love you, too, son. Got to go. I'll get your camel whip next time I get to the bazaar." *I do not want this uncertainty to touch your lives.*

I recall Nick Grimshaw, the gritty Bravo Company commander with perhaps the driest sense of humour of anyone I know, showing me some of the photographs and possessions they had found after one of their many clashes with Taliban forces. Nick's company spent most of the tour in the volatile Zhari and Panjwayi Districts. Bravo Company was in contact with the enemy seemingly all the time and our convoys were frequently taking new vehicle doors and windows out to his group. Grimshaw always impressed me with his poise and grace under fire. The photos he showed me were hero shots of young Taliban warriors, probably taken in Quetta, Pakistan, given the beautiful background scenery of the outdoor shots. The photos were chilling. They reminded me of those antique ambreotype and *carte de visite* photographs so prevalent among soldiers on both sides of the U.S. Civil War. They showed young men drummed up to fight, visibly infused with a familiar patriotism. The young warriors, like young men the world over, seemed intoxicated with the romance of their struggle, with the resolve of their courage. They were handsome young people barely to the right of childhood. Who could hate these young men? I don't. I don't hate the Taliban, but I hate the big bully fundamentalism they stand for. In their eyes they see themselves as the lifeblood of the insurgency, the true heroes of Afghanistan.

I was reminded of these grimy photos taken from Taliban warriors when watching one of my boys dolled up as a medieval warrior for Halloween in October 2006. I had been home less than a month and Kandahar was very much still with me that first October. I was still sweating the ammunition situation and flogging myself daily. We had gone to Value Village to pick up the kid's costumes and hardware on the way up to Ottawa to speak at General Hillier's CDS Seminar in late October. Aidan had wanted an expensive knight's kit that came with a plastic chest, a huge and elaborate sword, and a shield. I watched him try on his suit of armour in a hotel room in Hull, Quebec, as I prepared for my meeting at the CDS forum. He admired the rippled abdomen the close-fitting plastic armour gave him in the mirror and felt the easy, comfortable weight of the sword in his hand. He was so full of satisfaction and pride with his rubber weapons and the overall fit of the military costume. I could not help thinking to myself, "Are we really so different? Do any of our young men not harbour romantic notions of far away wars?" There is something alluring in fundamentalism that attracts the pilgrim soul of the young warrior. I saw it in Grimshaw's captured photos as surely as I see it on my son's face. There must be a way to protect our idealistic young people from the darkness. To me this is what our campaign in

Afghanistan is truly about — bringing a candle into a dark house. Tolerance deserves to win out over fundamentalism, but the mistake so many of us make is that the war against intolerance begins here at home in our schools, our institutions, and in our homes.

6 June 2006: Back from leave in Canada. D-Day.

7 June 2006: Rocket attack last night on the Base. One round landed north of the airfield near our ammo compound. No one hurt. No secondary attack. I feel edgy, unprepared. I have got to get a grip ... miss the kids, Martha ...

You must let go of them. If you want to see them again, if you want to be useful rather than lethal to your troops, you must let go. Even thinking about that mental readjustment after my 2006 theatre leave makes me nauseous. I may be a good officer or a good father, but surely I can't be both at the same time over here. I realized that night in June that I had to deaden my recollection of home and quickly. Thinking about how much and how rich life is at home is dislocating. It is ironic. They are the very reason I came to Afghanistan in the first place.

— Lieutenant-Colonel John Conrad,
Kandahar Diary, June 2006

15

Fighting Friction

"Christ. There goes 1 PPCLI launching another combat team into the slaughterhouse. What a fuckin' bozo."

The comment wafts over to my side of the command post during our evaluation exercise. It is a freezing cold morning in Wainwright, Alberta, in the fall of 2005 and our Task Force is on the attack. The remark is from one of the observer controller officers, a major, assigned to us to help the unit achieve the coveted status of operationally ready — opred. Your unit must be declared opred before you can deploy overseas. His loud opinion brings my blood to an instant boil.

"Hey, you!" I explode, being intentionally rude. "You get the hell out of here and stay the fuck out."

This kind of help we don't need. I made damn sure my entire command post understood that the task force he was criticizing was ours. The people he was deriding were us. Others outside of 1 PPCLI can criticize and question, but we won't. We can't invite friction between our units. They are our brothers.

If they call for it, we will rip our underwear to get it to them. We will never complain and we will never force them to explain why they need something in Kandahar. We will move heaven and earth to make sure they will never be alone and never be without.

— Lieutenant-Colonel Conrad,
Kandahar Diary, June 2006

Everyone from the venerable military historian to the rawest RMC cadet knows about friction in war. I too have been long familiar with the rubs and irritants that come with modern operations. The frictions of Kandahar more closely resembled the sort of friction Clausewitz was trying describe in his writing. The operation in southern Afghanistan subscribes to incredible frictions. Lieutenant-Colonel Ian Hope, a friend I have known for most of my career, is a confident, self-possessed leader. We worked hard on keeping our two units in harmony — the supporting and the supported during the Kandahar operations and yet there were forces in constant play that could easily have put us at odds with each other. I recall having lunch with Lieutenant-General Gauthier, the commander of Canadian Expeditionary Forces Command (CEFCOM) on KAF, when he visited the mission area in early June 2006. Expeditionary command is the superior headquarters for all deployed Canadian operations the world over and in this very real respect; General Gauthier was my boss's boss. He is a highly cerebral senior leader with an uncanny talent for the absorption and recollection of detail. He made an off-handed remark that really set me off.

"The battle group claims it gets very poor support from the NSE. Can you explain this?" My response to the general was admittedly a bit emotional, which is one of my greatest failings. The Canadian Army does not exactly relish emotion, and displaying too much of it will brand you as something less than professional. Me to a "T." I recall scoffing that the comment did not deserve his consideration as 1 PPCLI had in the NSE an administration company on steroids: an integral logistics capability that could see with fidelity all the way to the Port of Montreal from the most remote corners of Regional Command South. The greatest problem with the petite size of the NSE was in keeping up with our static yet crucial logistics functions on the camp. In short, we were too small, but not at the expense of battle group support. The NSE's main effort was 1 PPCLI, if we were going to do a shitty job somewhere, it would be on the camp or somewhere between KAF and Canada but never, ever beyond the wire. General Gauthier raised an eyebrow and made an almost imperceptible nod, not revealing in the act whether I had just confirmed in his mind what a damn fool I was or if he accepted my point. I left dinner feeling oddly dislocated and intensely worried. This feeling of distant scrutiny and dissatisfaction from unseen superiors at home stayed with me for the rest of my time in Kandahar.

When the CEFCOM commander left Afghanistan, I was peppered with questions and hand-wringing concerns from a number of different staff officers in Canada. Some of them were from General Gauthier's staff and some from the logistics focused Canadian Forces Support Command. In answering one of the many concerned queries from officers back home, my frustration got the better of me and I made a remark that came back to haunt me. In an email note to the Army G4 (the principal staff officer logistics), I flippantly stated that the battle group was well catered to for support and any shortfalls had our full and complete attention. I concluded my note by quipping that any complaints against our support from the battle group of this nature were without real substance and merely the results of the battle group whining. I regretted the remark. It was used to placate the senior officers in Ottawa, who sensed trouble in the logistics support of the fighting force. The remark in my email made it to Hope in a matter of hours. Ian was furious and he called me at my headquarters the next evening. In a few terse, intense sentences that I elect not to put down here, he said enough to make me feel worse than awful for my remark. I immediately walked up to Task Force Orion headquarters and forced my way into Hope's office. I found him drooped in his rarely used desk chair, rumpled maps and mundane staff work littering the desk of his plywood panelled sepulchre. Ever-present cigars, bits of ash, and a couple of General Hillier's coveted CDS coins left behind from our top commander's recent visit also lay on the desk. The commander of Task Force Orion looked old and drawn. I tossed him a replacement pair of ballistic glasses to fill in for a pair lost in the north. I apologized for what I had written and explained my frustration and how I had come to be in the mindset to say it in the first place. I told him about the comment on poor support that I had received from Lieutenant-General Gauthier and Hope was quick to assure me that it was neither his view nor the view of his company commanders. In fact, our collaboration in the difficult operation had gone well from the perspective of 1 PPCLI. Over the course of the next two hours we spoke about history, family, unit problems, tactical events, the U.S. Civil War, and eventually the issue itself. Ian had said nothing to General Gauthier or anyone else on the CEFCOM staff about the logistic support his battle group was receiving. I do not know where General Gauthier had heard the caustic remark, nor does it matter. The point is that friction between headquarters and units, friends, and colleagues exerts a tremendous pressure on a fighting force. Over the course of the year in Afghanistan I have grown protective of Ian. We have had some real fights and arguments and have not seen eye to eye on everything. I have shared the very blackest of nights with Ian and weighed the meanings of death and fear while staring through cigar smoke into the Afghan star rise. We also struggled with incredible frictions that swirled between our two units like a poison throughout the tour. Another infantry friend of mine, a colonel also with the Patricias, once remarked to me that Ian has the unassailable courage of his convictions. This sense of deep self-assuredness has earned Ian Hope some enemies, but I am not one of them. I will make no claim here to the historian's objectivity. As time marches on, the echoes of rumour and innuendo will continue to swirl around hard facts about Ian Hope and his battle group, but Ian is like a brother to me. A battalion commander in the army has a tight peer group with whom he or she can let down his hair. In a war zone like Kandahar I found that a brother commander is even more highly prized.

Another element of friction prominent on our tour was the whole inside the wire/outside the wire psychology. Certain aspects within the battle group cultivated this brand of elitism and it perplexed me as a senior leader in the task force. The "in the rear with the gear" mentality poorly applies in the contemporary operating environment. Everyone in that battle space was subject to attack. KAF itself was rocketed over 45 times during the tour and one Canadian narrowly escaped death from a 107 mm rocket attack while eating supper at the KAF kitchen. Such is the nature of the lava lamp battlefield. We lost soldiers from the medical corps and the NSE on the tour and I worked hard to shelter my unit from the "outside the wire" nonsense. It was particularly hard with Captain Bobby Alolega's supply organization that was largely camp-based by necessity. Their efforts were vital to our success. They were every bit as crucial as my convoy soldiers — the teams in the transport, repair, and recovery platoons. Elitism has its useful corners but when nurtured in non-contiguity it has a corrosive effect. There were no bigger fans of the 1 PPCLI Battle Group than the NSE in Kandahar. I would never have tolerated a derisive word from my principal staff or NCO cadre that would portray 1 PPCLI in a negative light. I am not sure how well this particular two-way street was travelled by others.

Friction exists between allies in a multinational operation. One must be on guard always to resist the lazy road to prejudice and passing judgment on a friend. It takes a tremendous amount of tolerance and patience to do this when you are tired or afraid or both. One of Canada's strategic goals was to deliver the NATO transition in the difficult south. To me, a simple logistics commander, this translated into working with the all of our allies at KAF and making the best representation possible for our country. The Brigade J4, Lieutenant-Colonel Jerome Delieu from the Netherlands, was the principal staff officer for logistics in General Fraser's headquarters. Both of us are logistics lieutenant-colonels working on the same mission and I became very good friends with this giant Dutch officer as the days went by. Lieutenant-Colonel Delieu was a "take charge" sort of individual who lacked perhaps discretion on what sort of things he should indeed take hold of. KAF for example, received some 70 to 90 civilian logistic trucks a day through its main gate to satisfy the logistic requirements of Regional Command South. When a security conundrum prevented the normal flow through to occur, Jerome took it upon himself to go out to the main gate and take charge, directing traffic and forcefully proffering his opinion to any soldier or Pakistani driver within earshot. No doubt a cathartic experience, but probably not the best place for a big brain like his to be tied up. Jerome found himself one day full of his own frustration and misguided sense of urgency barging into my command post and giving loud orders to my Canadian staff. Captain Heather Morrison, my smart-as-a-whip operations officer, nodded tactfully and absorbed everything the passionate Dutch giant was telling her to do and then made her way to Major McKenzie to explain the extraordinary thing that had just occurred. When Scott McKenzie briefed me on this, the first inclination was to strike out, get angry. I chose to take a soft approach on this one. I decided to give ground and I took Jerome for a coffee. We talked about his father-in-law in the Netherlands who had narrowly cheated death after a serious heart attack and now after the miracle of a timely bypass operation was doing just fine. We spoke on the big upcoming Operation Mountain Thrust and the sort of logistic tapestry we wanted to weave for the brigade and what I could offer from the Canadians. As we were parting, I asked him about the incident that had fired him up so much as to drag him into my operations room.

"Jerome, I'm disappointed that you would take the time to come to the Canadian NSE and not at least drop in to say hello." It was enough.

He was so chagrined and embarrassed in his tone that I felt a bit sorry for this decent bear of a man. I knew the calibre of the man. I knew that his big heart was always in the right place. To defeat friction, however, one has to be humble enough to take the rough with the smooth. The acknowledgement of friction and its stressors helps I think to make the right choices. There was nothing to be gained by embarrassing my fine Dutch colleague or giving him a blast of shit. For the entire tour, we received the highest support from the Brigade J4 staff. This friction will require unit leaders to recognize it as a phenomenon, work hard to reduce its corrosive effect, and be prepared to put anger and ego aside and give ground to neighbours.

> I can tell you the look on the ANA soldiers' faces when they were handed a new pair of boots was something else. This kind of thing will go a long way toward Canada getting a good name with the local government and soldiers, and everything we do toward getting them better prepared and equipped to take over security of their own country is one more step to CA forces coming home for good. It's part of the other elements to this mission (development and governance) that don't make exciting articles in the paper, but in the end are even more important that our beating the Taliban down.
>
> — Major Scott McKenzie, "Afghanistan Updates"

The donation of Canadian supplies to the 205 Corps Afghan National Army became a pet project of the NSE. The intent was to partner with the Afghan army as much as possible. Their logistics units were trained to sustain a state-of-the-art combined arms force when in reality they were fielding a gutsy 1950s style army. The logistics skill sets they required were far more basic, along the lines of immediate battlefield recovery, repair, and replenishment. My unit was too small and too busy supporting the Canadian mission in Kandahar to really take on the full vision I had for training the ANA logistics corps but we were able to make a meaningful donation of *matériel* to the 205th Corps. I still remember shaking hands with the corps commander, General Raouffi, as I passed over to him two sea containers full of pristine, but dated combat gear. I

The NSE presents two sea containers full of Canadian personal equipment to the G4 (logistics chief) of the 205th Corps, Afghan National Army (ANA). I still remember the earnest words of the corps commander: "General Fraser said he would get equipment for my soldiers. He has done so. General Fraser is my friend." The ANA in our time was not yet well versed in larger level army operations. Fighting at anything larger than company level was rare. However, the bravery and earnestness of the ANA was never in doubt. These soldiers serving in Afghanistan's most trusted institution are brave and steeped in combat experience.

was touched by his heartfelt expression of thanks. "General Fraser said he would get equipment for my soldiers. He has done so. General Fraser is my friend." The donation was modest in contrast to the money and effort that the United States has poured into the Afghan National Army since the fall of the Taliban regime, but it was by no means an empty gesture by our government. I felt the impact of deeds over words as we drove from Shirzai back to KAF.

I became good friends with U.S. Army Lieutenant-Colonel Brad Kohn who was the head adviser to the First Brigade of 205th Corps, the brigade garrisoned across from KAF at Camp Shirzai. Kohn was an avid Starbucks coffee fan. We spoke at FOB Martello about the kiwis he was able to grow on his West Coast acreage and how good it is to grow your own food. I made it clear to Brad that even though the Canadian logistics unit was small, we wanted to do everything in our limited means to assist the First Brigade in its operations with 1 PPCLI and in its development as part of the most trusted institution in Afghanistan. I received a note from Kohn in late July during the final overtures of Operation Mountain Thrust with a plea for fresh rations for the Afghan troops:

> John,
> General Mohammed is anxious to know if the Can-
> adians will buy fresh food for his troops. The point of
> contact for 1st Brigade is the XO [Executive officer]
> Colonel Ahmad. He can receive monies and supervise
> the purchases. Col. Ahmad is currently in the field fight-
> ing with Task Force Orion.
> — LTC Brad Kohn, U.S. Army

We had known from our experiences with the Afghan National Army operating with "A" Company out of Martello that their taste for the Halal hard rations was extremely limited. They preferred fresh goat meat and foodstuffs that were purchased locally wherever they operated. I made sure their preferences were met.

Brad,

Got your note. Please assure General Mohammed that money for purchase of fresh rations on behalf of 1st Brigade soldiers is en route tonight to Zhari District Centre. This has my full attention. My DCO will deliver it personally as he is attending LCol Hope's O-Group there this evening. Who can fight on an empty stomach?
— Lieutenant-Colonel John Conrad,
Canadian Forces, Kandahar

Deeds and not words rule the day in Kandahar. It is important to create the impression of having lots and being supportive even when you are constrained by limited assets as we were. It is equally important in my book to ensure Canada is well represented by us and that we never looked overly bookish or cheap when favours were asked of us. How we deal with our partners in the coalition must at least be as important as the example of tolerance we wish to hold up to Afghanistan. The moral impact on our friends and neighbours both in NATO and in the international community was vital in my judgment. Scott delivered the money to the hands of the LAV company commanders that same evening. A small act in the physical plane but the difference in the minds of our Afghan brothers and American friends was impossible to measure.

I recall a training film that I was shown as a young officer on the importance of teamwork inside an alliance like NATO. General Dwight D. Eisenhower was featured in the training segment and he lectured hard on the need for co-operation and teamwork between nations in the alliance. It seemed to me to be a very simplistic concept for such a highly decorated and accomplished commander to have to promote. Teamwork? Hell, is that not pretty obvious? Of course, what General Eisenhower knew from years of experience in the Second World War and as a NATO commander after the war was that military operations, particularly inside an alliance, are subjected to crushing frictions and irritants. His speech in that training film has stayed with me all my career. I did not understand it until Kandahar. Operations in Afghanistan submit themselves to incredible pressures, pressures that work to pull even solid teams apart. Friction at times put me at odds with both my battle group commander and friend, Ian Hope, and the Multinational Brigade chief of logistics — the two men with whom I had to work closely. Identify it early and fight it always.

EPILOGUE

In going where you have to go, and doing what you have to do and seeing what you have to see, you dull and blunt the instrument you write with.

— Ernest Hemingway

Corporal "Killer" MacKinnon has dropped his nickname for good. The soft-spoken MacKinnon struggled mightily with the return to normalcy after the tour in 2006, the Taliban Summer. He nearly lost his family, a beautiful young wife and a sparkling newborn daughter. Corporal MacKinnon only started working at the big base in Edmonton again in the fall of 2007 nearly a year after redeployment from Kandahar. When we talk I can see the ghosts of other days in the corner of his eyes. The day, 3 March 2006, that Sergeant Pat Jones pulled him out of the burning Bison armoured vehicle with his melted holster never strays far from his thoughts.

Although he stuck with the convoy escort job for nearly six full months after the actions of 3 March 2006, Sergeant Jones never truly outdistanced his demons. I have tried connecting with him a few times and the most success I ever had was chatting with his wife. The day I spoke with her, Jonesy was out on the road taking his teenage daughter through a driving lesson. The remarkable Pat Jones is in the initial throes of retirement from the Canadian Forces. He will never put on his uniform again. He does not have to. Pat Jones has done enough.

Corporal Jared Gagnon, wounded so severely in the accident that claimed Raymond Arndt on 5 August 2006, miraculously survived. The amazing life-saving first aid he received from Sergeant-Major Miles of the Royal Canadian Regiment on Highway 4 coupled with his own strength and determination carried him through an incident that could have easily ended his life. He is leading a full life in Alberta, and the physical scars that remain are almost unnoticeable at a glance. He is a young man full of potential and talent with the entire world in front of him. I join his parents in being profoundly thankful for all of this.

Major Scott McKenzie will soon be able to pick up his pen and write a whole new edition of "Afghanistan Updates" for his beautiful wife, Catherine. McKenzie has landed a staff job as the G4 in our treasured 1 Brigade in Edmonton. He will serve with General John Vance's Canadian headquarters, which is slated to deploy to Kandahar in the fall of 2008. I can't think of Scott as a subordinate anymore; in fact, I stopped looking at him that way in the middle of our 2006 Kandahar tour. He will always be the more talented little brother in my mind's eye. His career in the Canadian Forces is bright indeed.

The Canadian Forces is one of Canada's most trusted institutions, a fantastic organization that emphasizes teamwork. This fact makes it all the more difficult to understand the cultural disdain for the logistic arm of our military. Disdain and disinterest nearly cost us dearly on Canada's return to combat operations. Three hundred is not many soldiers to achieve what needed to be done in southern Afghanistan in 2006. As I write this during the fall of 2007, combat operations in distant Helmand Province are no longer conducted by Canadian troops and yet the Canadian logistics unit being prepared to go into Kandahar with the task force rotation in January 2008 is comprised of some 450 troops — nearly 60 percent more soldiers than participated in the pioneering efforts of my tiny 2006 NSE. The NSE that will replace them in August 2008 will be nearly 250 soldiers larger than mine — close to double in size. These new NSEs also have a team of Canadian contractors on KAF to furnish additional logistics services.

The Canadian Forces achieved a great deal in 2006 — not the least of which was denying control of Kandahar City to the Taliban. Our country and our tiny army are growing up around us in Kandahar. However, the consideration logistics derives from the leaders of the army remains shockingly and inappropriately slim. Logistics is more than ever a combatant partner on the battlefield, a crucible for tactical success. Yet, there remain deeply rooted cultural biases in the Canadian Forces that caused logistic services to be overlooked initially in Kandahar. These biases manifested themselves in "fighting echelon" elitism that was truly incongruous in the contemporary operating environment. If we want to succeed in this sort of fight we cannot push the loggies away. We need each other to survive in this contemporary battle space. We were extremely fortunate to succeed with the tiny combat logistics battalion we sent to the fight in February 2006. I know that our combat logistics troops carried a terrific physical and psychological burden on our behalf. In going back to war, we really underestimated the logistic support requirement that a counter-insurgency demands. We succeeded in 2006 because the young men and women who fill the logistic ranks in the Canadian Forces are among the best in the world at what they do. They are mentally tough and technically superb. More important, I found them to be both discerning and compassionate while treading on Afghan soil. The men and women with whom I served refused to lose. Kandahar represents Canada's most dangerous military mission since Korea. Even though our soldiers had not been involved in a sustained fight for generations, they met the challenge of Afghanistan, making sure that convoys would run, mail and supplies would flow, vehicles would get fixed in the centre of an infantry battle, and hamburgers would get flipped underneath barrages of mortar fire and rocket-propelled grenades, not because of any genius on my part or the part of the army staff or the headquarters in Ottawa but only because *they* willed it to be so. The projection of national power, the currency used to purchase the government's aims, has to be delivered by combat soldiers and underwritten by robust logistics troops. As proud as I am of the accomplishments of 1 PPCLI and the fine Canadian infantry battle groups that have followed it, my heroes in Kandahar will always be those noble troops that lumbered north in 16-ton logistic trucks, Bison repair vehicles, aftermarket armoured wreckers, and the like — no regimental bluster, no glitter, just sheer guts.

Your Canadian Forces are made up of soldiers, sailors, and airmen and women from across this great country. They are your own sons,

daughters, friends, and neighbours. They have different roles and functions inside the force from infantry through to personnel selection. The
ones that deliver logistics have a specific, time-revered role. The value of
their contribution has diminished in the in the eyes of some across the
breadth of Canadian military history, but I tell you now the esteem they
have earned and deserve could not be higher. The combat logistics troops
I knew are among the finest Canadians I have had the privilege of meeting. As an officer, a father, and as a taxpayer I am so very proud of them.
These soldiers have been measured by Canada's enemies on the contemporary battlefield around Kandahar and have been found not wanting.
They know all about the hell where youth and laughter go. In point of fact
they have been there many times.

This is what I learned from the thunder.

NOTES

1. The civilian airport terminal with its instantly recognizable arches is not used by the military. In 2006 this distinctive building, the symbol of the Kandahar Airfield, was being prepared for civilian-traffic use.

2. Canadian Forces drivers belong to the trade Mobile Support Equipment Operators — quite a handle. The soldiers of this trade prefer to be known as truckers because of the range of equipment and specialty vehicles they drive.

3. Accessed online at *http://en.wikipedia.org/wiki/Logistics#Origins_and_definition*.

4. Ian Malcolm Brown, *British Logistics on the Western Front 1914–1919* (Westport, CT: Praeger, 1998), 110.

5. Shane Schreiber, *Shock Army of the British Empire: The Canadian Corps in the Last 100 Days of the Great War* (New York: Praeger, 1997), 38.

6. Library and Archives Canada [henceforth LAC], RG9, Series III-d-2. Canadian War Diaries, 4th Canadian Division, 3 August 1918.

7. Schreiber, *Shock Army*, 37.

8. Accessed online at *http://en.wikipedia.org/wiki/Canada*.

9. Desmond Morton, *A Military History of Canada* (Edmonton: Hurtig Publishers, 1985), 92.

10. *Ibid.*, 106.

11. John English, *Lament for an Army: The Decline of Canadian Military Professionalism* (Toronto: Irwin Publishing, 1998), 19.

12. I think the magnitude of Canadian losses in this war takes generations to be fully absorbed and only now, as we close in on the 100th anniversary of its start in August 1914, are we really gaining the necessary perspective to appreciate fully the effects of the First World War on our country.

13. Brown, *British Logistics*, 139. A professional appreciation of the Canadian Corps' logistic achievements is best grounded on a review of the respective

staffs and line units that directly impacted its logistic architecture. The Canadian Corps logistics architecture was integral to the larger framework of the BEF. At the operational level the BEF logistics staff was divided into three different branches of the general headquarters (GHQ): an adjutant general branch (AG Branch), an inspector general communications (IGC), and a quartermaster branch (Q Branch). The AG Branch handled such specific sustainment issues as personnel, casualties, medical, and sanitary services. The IGC oversaw the management of all traffic on the LOCs from the seaport to the fighting corps. The quartermaster general (QMG) commanded the Q Branch and was responsible for the replenishment of the field force. Each level below the GHQ had a smaller, corresponding logistics staff centred on the QMG Branch that covered all logistics concerns. For example, a deputy adjutant and quartermaster general (DA and QMG) presided over the sustainment at the corps level. The Canadian Corps was blessed with a talented British DA and QMG, General G.J. Farmar, whom General Arthur Currie retained in that post through to the end of the war, despite the growing competencies of senior Canadian logisticians. Assistant adjutants and quartermasters general (AA and QMGs) were the senior Q officers in the divisions.

Like the corresponding levels of staff, logistics units became progressively smaller and more mobile the closer they got to the front. Army level units included the static organizations that operated the ports, warehouses, and railways (both heavy and light). The sinews of army support units ended at the forward railheads. From here, corps units would move the supplies forward to designated refilling points from which divisions would draw. In the Canadian formation, these corps level logistics assets were mechanical transport companies. Here indeed is the first peculiarity of the Canadian Corps. Certainly trucks at the corps level were a luxury not common to all corps of the BEF. Initially, Canada operated two types of corps mechanical transport units: the Ammunition Park and the Supply Column. The former, of course, hauled all of the Corps' ammunition, and the latter was charged with hauling all other classes of supply. A unit called the divisional train anchored logistics in the various Canadian divisions. The divisional trains moved *matériel* to the forward brigades from the refilling points established by corps resources. They were equipped with horses and wagons to meet the mobility challenge close to the fighting. The divisional train proved to be so resilient in structure and concept that Canada would never truly move away from it.

14. Malcolm Brown, *British Logistics,* 110.

15. Gervais Phillips, *Haig: A Great Captain,* accessed at *http://www.lib.byu.edu/-rdh/wwi/comment/haig1.html.*

16. Peter Wilson, ed., *Canadian Railway Troops During World War I, 1st Battalion Canadian Overseas Construction Corps, November 1917–April 1918, Volume One* (Campbellford, ON: Wilson's Publishing Company, 1995), 5.

17. Brown, *British Logistics,* 142.

18. C/JC/CPT 303/LE-30. Canadian Forces College lecture on Theatre Level Administration.

19. Brown, *British Logistics,* 146. Of this figure, 100,000 tons were available in France (timber and road stone for the most part). The delta, some 190,000 tons, would need to flow through the strategic replenishment system.

20. Lieutenant-Colonel Ian McCulloch, "A Study in Operational Command: Byng and the Canadian Corps," in Allan English's *The Changing Face of War* (Montreal and Kingston: McGill-Queen's University Press, 1998), 52.

21. *Ibid.,* 56.

22. Arnold Warren, *Wait for the Waggon: The Story of the Royal Canadian Army Service Corps* (Toronto: McClelland & Stewart, 1961), 19. General Buller was a highly respected combat arms officer in his own right. Upon appointment as the British Army's quartermaster general in 1887, Buller sought to solidify the transportation service of the British Army in his proposal for a fully combatant transportation arm — the Army Service Corps.

23. Jeffrey Williams, *Byng of Vimy* (London: Leo Cooper, 1983), 36. The author is also indebted to Dr. Chris Madsen of the Canadian Forces College for the background information on the primacy of LOCs in the Boer conflict and Byng's familiarity with their criticality.

24. Williams, *Byng of Vimy,* 146.

25. Schreiber, *Shock Army,* 21.

26. *Ibid.,* 21.

27. G.F.G. Stanley, *Canada's Soldiers 1604-1954: The Military History of an Unmilitary People* (Toronto: Macmillan of Canada, Third Edition, 1974), 328.

28. *Ibid.,* 329. It has been said that quantity has a quality all its own. This tongue-in-cheek axiom would appear to apply to the Canadian Corps.

29. English, *Lament for an Army,* 17.

30. Schreiber, *Shock Army,* 22.

31. *Ibid.,* 38.

32. *Ibid.,* 31.

33. The resulting new corps units were 1, 2, 3, and 4 Division MT Company as well as HQ MT Company for the support of corps troops. The Canadian Corps Supply Column and the Canadian Corps Ammunition Park — two distinct corps-level units — were fused into the Headquarters Canadian Corps Mechanical Transport (MT) Column. This new unit acted as the headquarters for five new subordinate MT companies. Similar to the amalgamation at their column headquarters, the respective divisional ammunition parks and divisional supply columns supporting each of the four divisions were amalgamated to form four new divisional MT companies.

34. Schreiber, *Shock Army*, 26. See also English, *Lament for an Army*, 16, for comments on sterling government support for the Canadian Corps and the benefit of maintaining the corps as one large unit.

35. McCulloch, 56.

36. *Ibid.*, 56.

37. English, *Lament for an Army*, 18.

38. Lines of communication ran eastward from French ports like Boulogne toward the Western Front by rail. Closer to the front, light rail, trucks, and finally, the horse-drawn wagons of the divisional trains, were used. For a formation to succeed on any grand scale, the supply lines would need to stretch and remain responsive to more stretching. As ironic as it may sound, the problem facing logistics then was the same one we face in Kandahar — how to respond to movement of *matériel* on an evolving battlefield.

39. Our Hercules lift capacity was augmented by contracted civilian cargo jets that would arrive direct from Trenton, Ontario. This increased the capacity of our air bridge but never released us from a hard finite reality. Getting more of anything was always difficult.

40. D.J. Goodspeed, *The Road Past Vimy: The Canadian Corps 1914–1918* (Toronto: Macmillan of Canada, 1969), 153.

41. Major-General Sir Julian Thompson, *The Lifeblood of War: Logistics in Armed Conflict* (London: Brassey's, 1991), 49.

42. Warren, *Wait for the Waggon*, 45. The spectacular career of Colonel Pat Hennessey would furnish abundant material for a separate book. Hennessey and his accomplishments in logistics modernization are commemorated on the Simonds Theatre Wall of Honour at the Canadian Forces College in Toronto as well as at the former RCASC Training School at CFB Borden, Ontario. Colonel Hennessey was killed in action in Hong Kong in 1940.

43. The designation "Royal" for both the British and Canadian Army Service Corps wasn't given until 1919.

44. *Sixty Glorious Years* (London, ON: RCOC Diamond Jubilee Yearbook, 1964), 15.

45. Patricia Giesler, *Valour Remembered* (Ottawa: Supply and Services Canada, 1995), 2.

46. Stanley, *Canada's Soldiers*, 399.

47. *Ibid.*, 399.

48. 1 Canadian Division Headquarters was re-established in 1988 at Kingston, Ontario, with the intent that it would be the training platform for the army's three brigade groups. The return of 1 Canadian Division was regrettably short-lived. It is true that during the heady days of Canadian Forces Europe and 4 Canadian Mechanized Brigade Group, Canada's army served inside and around larger NATO formations. As well, during our Kandahar mission in 2006 we were part of a multinational brigade that in turn belonged to a U.S. division headquarters in Bagram (CJTF 76). However, in terms of having our own division as a basic Canadian structure, the age had passed.

49. Demi-official letter from Lieutenant-Colonel Pospisil to Lieutenant-Colonel Strain dated 1992, 1.

50. *Ibid.*, 1.

51. *Camp Gagetown Gazette*, 1963.

52. The Honourable Douglas S. Harkness, minister of defence. From an official statement released 9 January 1963. Unit Scrapbooks of 1 Service Battalion, Edmonton.

53. *Camp Gagetown Gazette*, 1963.

54. *Ibid.*, 92.

55. Directorate of History and Heritage (henceforth DHH), *Rendez-Vous 81* Post Exercise Report.

56. Christopher Thurrott, "Is It Time to Purge the Service Battalion from the Order of Battle?" *The Service Battalion Newsletter* (Fall 1994), 17.

57. Douglas L. Bland, *Chiefs of Defence: Government and the Unified Command of the Canadian Armed Forces* (Toronto: Brown Book Company, 1995), 219.

58. *Ibid.*, 219.

59. *Ibid.*, 219.

60. Gerald Porter, *In Retreat: The Canadian Forces in the Trudeau Years* (Toronto: Deneau and Greenberg, 1979), vii.

61. Minutes of the CSS Doctrine Meeting Held at the St. Hubert Officers' Mess, 0830, 22 January 1996.

62. Lieutenant-Colonel Al Morrow assisted the author with the search for the old minutes of these boards. Al was at the time a doctrine writer at the doctrine directorate of army headquarters. Thus far, the author hasn't found a single person at the Land Staff HQ who knows for sure where the minutes are filed or if they were even kept. The quote from the minutes at note 31 comes from papers collected by the author.

63. Soldiers of God. Kandahar is ancient Arabic for Alexander.

64. Martin van Creveld, *Supplying War: Logistics from Wallenstein to Patton* (Vail-Ballou Press, New York. 1977), 1–2.

65. Logistics planners pay attention to distance and time, as they impact how much fuel tends to get consumed, but more important they speak loudly about how long it takes to get more of any given commodity. I have made a living for myself with the simple math equation: distance equals speed multiplied by time (d=vt). In truth, this little mathematical certainty is all a competent officer really must know to be relevant and successful inside his army. Every soldier in the army must know how long it takes to get more. This is the least you should know about logistics.

66. Van Creveld, *Supplying War*, 151.

67. This final request for more support troops was tabled at an organization conference at 1 CMBG Headquarters in Edmonton just before Christmas Holidays on 9 December 2005.

68. This staff is now split between CEFCOM and CANOSCOM J4 staffs as part of CF Transformation.

69. This support was offered by Colonel J. Cousineau in early December 2005. Cousineau was serving on the DCDS Staff as J4 Logistics at the time. A TAV represents additional specialist soldiers who deploy to a theatre for short durations to assist with the completion of a discreet task. The task is generally of such size and complexity that it is beyond the scope of the in-place force to do it alone. I used supply TAVs to make basic *matériel* accounting possible in the theatre.

70. Master Warrant Officer Butters served the NSE and the battle group as the battle replacement for the RSM, Chief Warrant Officer Randy Northrup. Jim actually served as Task Force Orion RSM during Randy Northrup's leave period. Because of his dual roles Jim became a source of friction at times between the units, but the friction was worth it. He was never totally

comfortable as a member of a logistics unit, but what he brought to us was priceless. I never had a chance to thank him for his service with the NSE as my convoy was attacked on his last day in theatre on 22 July 2006. Jim left that night, and I never got back to KAF until the 23rd. Thanks, Sergeant-Major.

71. LAC, RG9, Series III-d-2. Canadian War Diaries, 1st Canadian Division War Diary, Report on Amiens Operations, 8 August to 20 August inclusive, 19.

72. *Ibid.*, 18.

73. Merchant ships destined to travel through the wolf packs of U-boats in the Atlantic during the Second World War would wait in the Bedford Basin by Halifax for the next fully armed and escorted convoy to head east across Atlantic.

74. The only exception to these figures was artillery ammunition. In the case of artillery, the weapon was used so selectively up to June that it was deemed better to have the battery commander tell us what sort of expenditures they considered reasonable over a longer period and build our holdings from there.

75. These operations in August 2006 took place during the handover between 1 PPCLI and 1 RCR, which called for some extra amounts of ammunition for priming the individual soldier's weapons as well as mission rehearsal training. The big piece that was to come early in the tour for 1 RCR was, of course, Operation Medusa.

76. In truth this desire to protect busy combat arms soldiers from worrying about matters of strategic supply was what caused the stressful ammunition conundrum with General Fraser. We worked so hard to fix the problem without bothering him that when it finally came to his attention it was all the more shocking. I still believe in the principle of owning the problem and fixing it away from the attention of our time-impoverished combat arms, but I know now how to better engage the boss when I am plying this skill.

77. Adnan R. Khan, "We Will Likely Take Casualties," *Maclean's*, Vol. 118, Nos. 27 and 28, 4 and 11 July 2005. Quoting Canadian Forces Captain Angus Matheson.

78. This was predicated using the average duration of most of the scraps that Task Force Gun Devil, the U.S. Army predecessors to 1 PPCLI, experienced in Kandahar Province during the previous year.

79. It took approximately 9,000 British servicemen and women to furnish the army-level support required by each of the Canadian divisions fighting in the Second World War.

80. Richard M. McMurray, *Two Great Rebel Armies: An Essay in Confederate Military History* (Chapel Hill: University of North Carolina Press, 1989), 70.

81. RSM Earles, the oldest boy in his family commenting on a difficult conversation with his mother. Pat's dad had passed away just before Christmas in 2005 about 45 days ahead of our deployment. His work in Kandahar was one subject that his mother could only deal with in glimpses.

82. My words for Master Corporal Raymond Arndt at his ramp ceremony at KAF.

INDEX